WALTHAM'S PEAK

Uplands

BETSY BOYD LESLIE

Illustrations by David H. Boyd

ISBN: 1516803701
ISBN-13: 978-1516803705

Lovingly dedicated to my parents,
David and Cynthia Boyd,
who rose above the vicissitudes of life.

CONTENTS

ACKNOWLEDGMENTS

I wish to express my deep gratitude
to the following individuals:

John, thank you for being a man of unquestionable integrity.

JR, Laura, Leah, and Laina Jane, thank you for your
patient waiting and confident support.

Dave, thank you for visually illustrating what I could not.

Lisa, Mom, Elizabeth, John, and Teresa, thank you for
critically reading and kindly critiquing.

Kelly and Teresa, thank you for your goliath
patience and valuable expertise.

Chapter 1

COMMENCEMENT

Today would mark the acquisition of Ian Campbell's final quarter million. Assuming the disheveled clerk hadn't found the documentation Ian had misfiled, and assuming Judge Allen hadn't developed a working knowledge of the Federal Rules, and assuming the prosecutor hadn't taken the time to calculate and compare dates, today's court appearance would be Ian's commencement, his graduation to early retirement.

Inching his long frame out of bed, he began his last morning work routine. Hair slicked, suit donned, and shoes shined, Ian sat down to his prepared fare. A French-pressed coffee was consumed with the day's *Wall Street Journal*.

In the background, a lovely, languid woman sponged counters and emptied the dishwasher. She glanced at Ian with every turned page, expectancy written on her face.

Ian drained his coffee, swirling the detritus as he pushed the emptied cup toward the woman. He assessed his tailored Fiorivanti for imperfections. Dressed for the part, there was no stopping Ian Campbell. His engaging persona and chiseled features went a long way in and out of court. Without looking up, he pronounced, "Today's the day, Kat!"

He finally glanced at the woman leaning against the

dishwasher, arms akimbo. Her expression revealed nothing, her tone even less.

"That's great, honey." She continued to stand and stare.

"I hope you got the tickets for the 3:35 to Raleigh. Would you be sure my galoshes make it into my carry-on? We might hit some rain when we get there." Ian dabbed his napkin to a moistness on his mouth.

"Yes, I booked the 3:35 flight. I already packed your galoshes," she responded.

"Perfect," he quickly grabbed his briefcase, pecked her cheek and walked to the door, "then I'll see you when I get out of court. We'll begin our new life tonight with a toast in front of a raging fire at Uplands. Oh yeah," he retreated a step, "be sure to leave a note for the maid."

"Yes, perfect," she repeated as the door closed behind him.

She surveyed the empty room. The kitchen opened onto a large living area. It contained a host of exquisite modern furniture. Sharp corners and industrial colors had made an impression on Ian while staying in a client's summer home in the islands. Due to Ian's prowess at finding loopholes, the client's racketeering charge had disappeared, and the money he hadn't laundered appeared in Ian's bank account. With one month's worth of island investigation and account scrutiny, Ian was half a million dollars closer to retirement and a living room suite closer to a penthouse.

"Honey, it feels more like a home. Not to mention that it's more affordable and comfortable," Kat had pointed out in an attempt to assuage Ian. "It's not a penthouse, it's a pretentioushouse. If you're so keen on moving, let's move into that cute bungalow on Clark, or even the brownstone on Beacon Hill. We could renovate that and make it look so elegant."

"Kat, I thought we'd agreed on the furniture. That furniture, already ordered and paid for, will not work in the cottage or the brownstone." His voice was sounding like the sneer on his face.

"I never agreed to anything, Ian. I recall you telling me that you *saw*

it, you *liked it, and* you *ordered it." The emphasis on "you" was gentle, but unmistakable. "I don't recall being a party to that transaction in any way, shape, or form."*

"Oh, come on, Kat. You're going to love it! The penthouse view of Boston Commons is spectacular. Besides, you'll settle in to the new look when you set foot in the studio I've been working on for you. You've been asking, and I'm delivering!"

The wiper blades swished, allowing the red light above them to blur into anonymity.

"Studio?" she repeated out loud. "I've asked for fifteen years through three moves and now you want to give me a studio?"

"I've already hired a designer to modify one of the bedrooms. We don't need it anyway. He'll make it look as though it was built with the house. You'll fit right in."

Kat stared out of the Mercedes, winking at the glare of oncoming headlights. She sat motionless, mute.

"Perfect! Then it's settled. We'll sign the contract on the penthouse next Wednesday. I've already had Shelly pencil in the time so she wouldn't schedule any court dates."

Kat untied her apron, folded it neatly and tucked it into a drawer. An hour later, she surveyed the suitcases she'd placed by the front door. She unzipped Ian's carry-on to make sure the galoshes were packed. Her slim fingers brushed a stray tendril of chestnut hair behind her ear. She made her way to the desk, pulled out the top drawer and selected some steel grey stationary, an anniversary gift from Ian. She took her seat and began to write.

A briefcase stood agape on the defense table in courtroom number twelve on the first floor of the Suffolk County Courthouse. Ian's Mont Blanc emblazoned his signature on a legal document.

A Fiorivanti sat next to him on a man in his fifties, Ian's client, Stephen Woodrow. The client's salt and pepper hair was immaculate. His manicure was recent. Mr. Woodrow's calm repose juxtaposed the official surroundings; he was remarkably comfortable considering.

"Mr. Campbell, I trust you brought your calendar today in order for us to set a trial date," huffed the judge from behind the bench.

"Yes, sir, I do have my calendar with me today. In light of the forms I've filed, I am assuming Mr. Ross will provide us a date within the week." Ian calmly looked over at the prosecutor. The prosecutor provided the look Ian had counted on: sheer panic.

"Sir," began Mr. Ross, as he leafed through the reams of paper before him, "I am assuming Mr. Campbell is referring to a Demand for Speedy Trial. However, our office has not received this form, nor has a courtesy call been placed to my secretary."

The judge's brow began to furrow as he peered over his bench to the clerk sitting beneath him.

"Ms. Timmins, would you please review your files in regard to this new development."

The stricken clerk licked her finger and feverishly began rifling through her file.

At the side of the room a door opened and shut. A stout, disheveled woman scurried to the judge's bench. She whispered something to him, stabbing her finger at the document she'd placed on the desk. While the judge cogitated on her secret information, he peered at the paper. The woman scampered out the door through which she had come. This time she was paperless.

Ian passively took in the clerk rifling, the judge peering and the prosecutor panicking. This was exactly what he had orchestrated. He had played by the rules, but exploited incompetence. "Zealously advocate" were the terms of his contract as a lawyer representing his client. He had exploited those terms straight to early retirement.

"Your Honor," offered the prosecutor with a nervous smile, "there is no record of the State having received this filing. Furthermore, the State is unprepared to present evidence in a jury trial in the next week. We are still in the process of discovery. The State believes that we will uncover far more than the one million dollar embezzlement charge, which has been filed. Ongoing investigations indicate that Stephen Woodrow embezzled five times that amount, your Honor. We simply need more time. Filing additional charges and preparing for this trial will take months beyond today."

The prosecutor gained momentum as he continued, "Sir, in light of the fact that no Demand has been filed according to statute, we ask for a continuance today and a waiver of Speedy Trial." The prosecutor exhaled. His shoulders relaxed. He sensed a catastrophe averted.

Ian picked up the document on the shiny expanse before him. "Permission to approach, Your Honor?" As he crossed the courtroom and handed the document to the clerk he commented, "Judge, as to why the State does not have a copy of my client's Demand for Speedy Trial, I cannot hazard a guess. However, I have just handed the Clerk my own copy of the Demand, stamped and dated the third of November of this year."

The judge glanced at the prosecutor, and stole a look at the clerk. He held up the document he'd been handed moments earlier. "Mr. Campbell, much to my surprise, I too, now hold such a stamped and dated document; Mr. Woodrow's Demand for Speedy Trial."

"Judge," piped up the flustered clerk, "I found it. The dates coordinate with those of Mr. Campbell's. Demand for Speedy is in effect, sir, and needs to be met within the week."

Ian retrieved his document from the clerk's debris and resumed his position at the great mahogany table.

"In response to Mr. Ross's comments, Judge, I would like to respectfully remind the court of the Federal Rules of Criminal Procedure."

At this juncture, Ian inadvertently read the nameplate affixed to the judge's bench: Judge Randall Allen. He smiled to himself. He had specifically and carefully ensured that *this* case would end up in front of *this* judge. The randomness, inherent in the system, did not apply to Ian Campbell. Choosing, arranging, and manipulating people were his forte; law was simply the medium in which it was utilized.

Judge Allen was notorious for being ignorant of the Federal Rules. More importantly, he was notorious for being insecure. In court, he frequently erred at the trial level, making him one of the most overturned judges at the appellate level in Suffolk County history. Although Judge Allen was aware of this fact, his voting public was not. He let the charade continue as he assuaged his guilt and fed his pride.

This was precisely the information Ian had counted on and precisely why he was standing before the most reversed judge in Suffolk County with a million dollar charge. Ian began his commencement address.

"According to eighteen U.S. Code, section 3161, and I quote, your Honor, 'Unless the defendant consents in writing to the contrary, the trial shall not commence less than thirty days from the date on which the defendant first appears through counsel or expressly waives counsel and elects to proceed *pro se*.'

Mr. Woodrow's date of first appearance was 24 days ago, Judge. My client's demand was timely filed, asking for his rights to be upheld within that thirty-day limit. In compliance with proper procedures, the Clerk's Office and Mr. Ross's office were both provided with a copy, albeit ones they did not locate until today."

Ian selected a file folder from his briefcase, and let it fall to the table. Placing his finger on the cover for emphasis, he continued.

"In response to Mr. Ross's commentary on filing new or additional charges, subsection H, 1, a through h, indicates all the exceptions that would provide leeway for the application of this rule. However, none of those apply." Holding up a new finger with enumeration, he continued, "No proceedings for mental competency have transpired. No examinations regarding physical capacity have transpired. No interlocutory appeals have been filed. No proceedings regarding the transference of the case have taken place. No pretrial motions have been filed. No transference delays have taken place. And although Mr. Ross has *considered* filing additional charges, that has not transpired either."

In any other courtroom he would not have bothered with the laundry list of statutory exceptions. In this courtroom, in front of *this* judge and prosecutor, he knew it would score remarkable intimidation points. He had counted on the insecure judge and overworked line attorney to play into his plans, their faults essentially doing his job for him.

If Mr. Ross happened to respond with statutory argumentation or caselaw, Ian was ready for that, too. The requisite materials and paperwork were situated safely beneath his Demand. However, he highly doubted that would be the response. Mr. Ross had admitted that he came to court fully expecting a simple Disposition Day in which they would schedule yet another Disposition Day. Such were the methods and madness of the overworked and underpaid government attorneys. Which was yet another reason it was so easy to misfile State paperwork.

"Judge," pleaded the stricken prosecutor, "we simply cannot be ready within the week for trial, especially in light of the holidays upon us. The Clerk's Office only has three days of the week scheduled for trial, and the following two weeks have been removed from the docket per the Court's request."

Being reminded of his paltry grasp of the rules and his penchant for vacation days in the same pre-trial motion had liquidated whatever patience Judge Allen had left.

"It appears to me, Mr. Ross, that you have one of three choices," his patience leaked out as he spoke. "You may either set this for trial, doing your best to represent the citizens of this state. Or, you may make Mr. Campbell's client a reasonable offer. Or, you may drop the charges and spare you and your office the embarrassment of taking an unprepared million dollar embezzlement charge to trial, giving the civil courts an opportunity to fill their dockets." He completed his list, removed his reading glasses and glared at the prosecutor as he awaited a response.

"Your Honor," responded the prosecutor, "I came to court today prepared to schedule a trial in the distant future and continue discovery …"

"That much is understood, Mr. Ross," boomed Judge Allen. "But if you'll give me a moment," the prosecutor was now fully grasping his position, the sweat beading on his brow. "I will review the file and make Mr. Woodrow an offer." He collapsed into his chair behind a box of files.

"With all due respect, Your Honor," offered Ian, "Mr. Woodrow and I are ready and willing to go to trial within speedy or agree to the charges being dropped. Mr. Woodrow is not amenable to an offer."

The prosecutor stared agape at the judge.

A veritable Athena in her green velour jacket and jeans, Kat strode to the kitchen counter where her purse lay open. In response to the doorbell, she pulled out her keys and slung her purse over her shoulder.

"Just a minute, Alfred!" she spoke to the door. She swept a final glance around the penthouse in the steps it took to reach the doorknob.

The door opened to reveal a grey-haired porter with cart in tow. His ready smile caused Kat to grin.

"Thank you, Alfred." She squeezed his right hand with her left and pulled the wrinkled doorman to her in a quick embrace.

"If you'd have the luggage downstairs and ready to place in a cab when Mr. Campbell arrives, I'd appreciate it." She handed him some cash and a key and held the door for him.

"Yes, ma'am, Ms. Katherine. I'll be sure to have these ready when you leave for the great white south!" He grinned again as he stood up with his load.

"You're the best, Alfred," and she leaned in and kissed him on his forehead.

The Fiovorantis stood in front of the double wooden doors marked "Courtroom 12."

"Mr. Campbell, I don't know how you did it, but I'm mighty impressed with what you've done for me," beamed Stephen Woodrow. "If you'd told me I'd be stepping out of here a free man today, with no trial, no jail time awaiting me, I would never have believed it." Mr. Woodrow extended his manicured hand. Ian gave it the requisite grasp.

"I'm just doing my job, Mr. Woodrow, meeting the terms of my contract. I'm glad you're pleased with the results. Enjoy your family this Thanksgiving, Mr. Woodrow, and be sure to give thanks for this country's great legal system." Ian turned to go.

"I'll be thankful five million times over, Mr. Campbell."

Ian hesitated a moment, but didn't turn back. His heels clicked as he marched down the marble hallway to the exit sign.

BETSY BOYD LESLIE

Chapter 2

ENIGMA

A cab pulled up and the doorman opened the door. The hem of the Fiorivanti appeared.

"Welcome home, Mr. Campbell. Did you have a good day in court?" Alfred asked as the rest of the suit emerged.

"Yes, thank you, a very good day indeed. Is everything set?"

"Yes, sir. Ms. Kat, er, Mrs. Campbell had me get your luggage ready to go and I've already arranged for a cab to the airport," Alfred beamed at Ian.

"Perfect. I'll change and be down subsequently." Alfred held the door as Ian disappeared through it.

The lock clicked and Ian strode into his penthouse. He stowed his briefcase in its usual location on a shelf in the hallway closet. Emptying the contents of his pockets on the kitchen counter, envelopes caught his eye. He picked up a steel grey envelope with Kat's handwriting on the front.

"Millie," Ian said out loud. "Good girl, Kat. You remembered the maid. And what have we here?" He put down the grey envelope and picked up a legal sized envelope with

"Ian" inscribed on the front.

As he tore through the narrow end and upended the envelope, an airline ticket and note fell out. Ian mumbled the contents out loud to the empty room.

Ian,

Congratulations on your final victory in court today! (Was there any doubt?)

Something has come up which may cause me to miss this flight. Please, don't wait for me.

Enjoy Uplands,
   Kat

Ian grimaced. He raked his fingers through his hair, glanced at his watch, and slapped the ticket on the counter. This wasn't part of his plan. Besides, what could Kat possibly have to do that was important enough to interfere with the culmination of his career? He didn't have time to argue, he had to shower.

Fifteen minutes later he emerged from the bedroom coiffed and dressed for travel. His finishing touch was the World War II bomber jacket Kat had given him for Christmas the year before. He grabbed his wallet, placed it in his back pocket, snatched up the airline ticket, tucked it inside his jacket, and took one last glance around before closing the door behind him.

Ian's leather carry-on slapped against his leg as the passengers jostled their way to baggage claim. He collected his and Kat's luggage, conscripting a porter to procure a warm cab and move his gear. With swift efficiency, the porter waved Ian into a cab while he and the cabbie filled the trunk.

"Where to, mister?"

"Mount Laurel."

"You got me there, mister." The cabbie proceeded to punch the information into his cell phone and sped away.

With his galoshes now comfortably securing his feet, his hands gloved and the cab parked at Uplands, he stepped onto the newly fallen snow. The gravel drive crunched beneath his boots. While the cabbie extricated his bags, Ian surveyed his work.

The beautiful edifice before him had been his brainchild. In the glow of the headlights his eyes traversed the stairs, a sweeping twelve-foot swath leading up to a thick wooden door. The jalousies in the top of the door limited the light, allowing nothing more than a thin strip. It needn't admit more, for the windows on the south side of the home stretched from floor to ceiling, allowing for a breathtaking twenty vertical feet of mountain vista. They flanked the large stone fireplace, which easily warmed the living area.

This side of the creation contained matching windows of more modest mien. They were ample for eying arriving visitors, but sufficiently sized to protect personal life. The latitudinal logs making up the walls were of such breadth they bespoke longevity; a longevity that was to see them through the years of ease ahead. Ian smiled to himself in approval.

"Give me a call when you're ready to head back to the airport, sir," the cab driver announced as he held out his hand. Ian filled it with cash.

"Will do." Ian was eager to be away from this man and into Uplands.

"They're calling for snow flurries tonight." He pointed to Ian's Range Rover sitting under the porte cochere. "If I were you, I'd hunker down for the night and get some extra supplies tomorrow. It's going to be a white winter, mister."

"Thanks for the advice." Ian dispatched the driver and pulled out his key.

"Uplands ~ Scotland in NC," was engraved on an oval brass placard from which his key now danced in the departing headlights. Kat had given it to him with a note that read, "Congratulations on your beautiful brainchild." And rightly so, thought Ian at the time.

He had scoured real estate magazines, architectural digests,

15

design sites, and virtual tours looking for the perfect features for his retirement villa. It was going to be his crowning achievement awaiting him when he'd made his final million.

Although an architect had been hired to draft the plans, he was merely the scribe. Ian was the creator. *Architectural Digest* and *Southern Living* got that right when they wrote their articles. Captions under inspiring photos of Uplands and its immediate environs, gave Ian all the credit. "A chalet of enduring excellence." "Simple in style, elegant in execution." Regardless of the periodical, they were complimentary of Ian's results.

He was immediately reminded of this fact as he turned to close the massive wooden door behind him. There was Kat in the most recent article, framed by the sweeping windows, leaning against the fireplace with a wineglass in her hand. Ian had the article framed in Campbell plaid and placed it on the table by the door: the first thing he saw as he entered. The caption under her visage read, "Kat Campbell, wife of the Uplands creator, Ian Campbell: At home in elegance."

He tossed his keys and wallet on the table as he retrieved the bags from the porch. Asking the cabbie to bring them in would have meant a lingering smell of stale smoke. In spite of the wheels, Ian carried each bag across the living room and up the stairs to the master bedroom. He didn't want any of his three thousand square feet of imported Macassar Ebony marred.

A quick inspection of the three bedrooms, two baths and sitting area upstairs indicated all was well. He unpacked his suitcases, refolding and placing his clothes in their compartments in his custom closet. The emptied suitcases were put away. Kat's full bags were left in her closet for her to tend to when she arrived.

Given the hour, Ian selected some flannel pajamas and wool slippers, slipped into the glass enclosed shower and soaped away the day.

Before indulging in a warm fire, Ian inspected the bottom floor. Living area inviting. Mudroom uneventful. Dining area immaculate. Kitchen well-stocked.

Incessant growling reminded him he hadn't eaten since

lunch. The next task at hand was to find something quick to eat with his evening toddy. He was glad he'd arranged for his maid to tend to a few things prior to his arrival. Each opened cupboard revealed precisely what he had requested.

Crackers, cheese, smoked salmon, and a glass of wine later, Ian sat before a roaring fire, the cares of a hectic career and misplaced madness behind him. He got up to check his phone for a text from Kat. She usually didn't text him. Shelly, his office administrator, was the only one to bother communicating with him via text. He never checked them outside of work-related events, and had made that clear to Kat.

Kat's absence was beginning to concern him. He pushed some buttons on his phone, saw nothing new and carried his dishes back to the kitchen.

Indeed, his change of address had taken effect. A large, neat pile of missives by the refrigerator indicated as much. A glance at the mail revealed local pizzeria coupons, health clinic flyers and house cleaning ads. His thumb landed on a familiar script. He furrowed his brow and tore open the narrow end of the envelope. Unlike the steel grey notes she used for personal correspondence, this stationary was large with elaborate illumination framing lovely letters.

Dear Ian,

By the time you read this, you will have reached your beloved Uplands. I won't be coming.

Twenty years is a long time. During that time, I have successfully become invisible to you. So successfully, in fact, that I was becoming invisible to myself. That cannot be a good thing for either of us. I was no more than an Alfred, Millie or Shelly to you, doing your bidding, enabling your career and adorning your creations.

Had you taken me in your arms any time this past week and asked my opinion or input on anything to do with our future, I would have called the Uplands maid and asked her to retrieve this letter.

I would have come to Uplands and spent the rest of my life with you. Since invisibility ruled the day, I didn't make the call and you're reading this letter.

I thought I "got" the math of marriage: the two of us were to become one. Naively, I presumed that would work out to your better half and my better half coming together to make one whole person. I even assumed that sometimes that might work out to 75% plus 25% equaling 100% when you or I were going through personal struggles. What I was not expecting was that all of Ian and none of Katherine would equal one happy marriage.

Squelching my personal desires and gifts was the unsatisfactory result. Initially, I considered each of these a victory. A victory in that I was able to suppress my desires and allow you to achieve yours. We were one, were we not? Your victories were mine, and all that sort of thing? As I look back, I can see that ultimately the sum total of these so-called victories was failure. I enabled you to mistreat me and those around you. I allowed you to make me invisible. That was wrong.

In spite of it all, I still love you, Ian. It is because of that truth that I have not followed you to Uplands. That place is yours. That idea was yours. That dream was yours. I haven't the wherewithal to change you, our marriage, or myself on your turf, especially that turf. I need to start over and figure out who I am without your giant persona and our old habits ever about me. I am setting myself free.

I have enclosed divorce papers and an addressed envelope to my attorney's office. Simply sign the papers and send them out in tomorrow's mail. My attorney will do the rest. You need not worry, Ian. I have asked for nothing. You may keep everything. None of it was ever mine anyway.

With much love and great sadness,
Katherine

Thirty minutes later, Ian was sound asleep deep in the leather couch, clinging to a bottle of Scotch with one hand and Kat's letter in the other.

Chapter 3

ROOM SERVICE

The pounding in his head woke Ian. He dismissed both the heavy hitting metronome and the clinking accompaniment in the background. Perhaps he could wash them both away with a dark roast. He stumbled to the bathroom, steadying himself at the doorway. He didn't bother to close the door, but he did flush. Unsanitary, Ian was not. The pounding and clinking continued.

Attempting to ignore the assaults to his senses, Ian grimaced, closing his eyes tightly from the sun steeling in the windows. He stepped into the kitchen, reaching for the fridge to steady himself. Instead, to his utter astonishment, the opened refrigerator door closed behind his weight, and Ian lost his balance.

To Ian's utter astonishment, a young woman stood in the light from the fridge. He almost fell into her, as he mentally reconfigured the placement of the fridge and grabbed the now closed door.

"Bacon 'n eggs," muttered the girl. Her short brown hair brought her to a full height of five foot two. Her simple face fed him a smile as she took the egg carton back to the stove. Pans placed, coffee brewing, eggs cracking – no wonder he'd heard background noises. They hadn't all come from his bottle of Scotch.

Forced to sit, Ian slid into a chair and looked around. "Who are you?" he asked, more for confirmation of reality than a desire to know the girl's name.

"Emma. My name Emma," she offered while cracking eggs into a pan.

Ian flinched with each new crack, each new pan movement. He held his head in his hands. The stranger was curing his hangover faster than a dark roast would any day. She set a Campbell plaid coffee cup in front of him and poured warm brown liquid into his cup. The clang of the carafe being returned to its seat caused Ian to jump. A pint of half-and-half was placed before him. The smell of the roast was beginning to enliven Ian.

"No sugar?" Emma shared with a thick tongue.

"What?"

"No sugar," Emma repeated with a sweeping gesture to the counter top.

Without thinking, Ian provided, "Sugar's in the first cupboard. Red bin."

Emma quickly stirred the eggs, then made her way to the indicated cupboard. Having located the red bin, she pushed it in front of Ian, crowding him to sit up. Drawers were pulled out and pushed in. After finding a spoon, she placed that with the rest of the assemblage.

Squinting his eyes and stirring his coffee, he muttered, "Who are you? What are you doing here?"

"Emma. Emma make bacon 'n eggs for breakfast." She was dumping bacon on a plate and placing it in the microwave. With her thick fingers, she pushed button after button and stood staring at the uncooperative appliance.

"New 'wave," she announced, "how make start?"

"Did Rosa ask you to come here this morning and provide room service or something?"

"No."

"Did Mrs. Campbell hire you?"

"No."

"Then what the hell are you doing here?" It hurt to yell, the echoes were still resounding in Ian's head.

"Emma make bacon 'n eggs." She looked at him patiently. "How make 'wave go?"

"Did my secretary, Shelly, ask you to do this?"

"No."

"My partners at the firm?" However unlikely that was, Ian was running out of explanations.

"No."

Her simplicity was baffling. Asking questions didn't get him anywhere. Between an emotional ambush and Scotch hangover, Ian was ill-prepared to handle the enigma standing before him. The most he could piece together was that something had been pre-arranged without his knowledge. Otherwise, how would she have gained admittance? Why would she innocuously be providing breakfast for him, a stranger?

With his head in his hands, trying to take in the situation, he turned to take in Emma. One thing he did have figured out was that this Emma person was not going away or being explained away until her agenda was complete. In his present condition, Ian had to acquiesce.

"Enter the time, press 'start' twice."

"Time," she repeated as she continued to stare at the machine. She pushed some more buttons randomly hoping for helpful results.

With each beep, Ian winced. "Stop, wait!" he barked. He held his right hand up to her in the universal crossing guard symbol while his left pushed him up from the table. He struggled over to the microwave. Punching three buttons with authority caused the microwave to whirr into action. Ian stumbled into his seat again. The microwave hummed while Emma pushed eggs around in the pan and Ian laid his head on the table.

Once more Ian tried to cross-examine his witness. "Who sent you? *Why* did they send you?" This time he added a little more umph and looked directly at her small face.

Emma stopped stirring and turned to answer him, "Emma make bacon 'n eggs for breakfast." She gave Ian a gentle smile with her information.

"Oh my god," Ian groaned as he let his face fall into his hands again.

"Yes, thank God when eat bacon 'n eggs," agreed Emma.

Temporary capitulation was required. Ian began adding ingredients and stirring carefully until his coffee took on the right hue. He tasted it. Emma clinked and clanked until bacon and eggs appeared on the table in front of Ian.

More banging provided Ian with a plate and fork. Emma sat down next to Ian. She placed her thick hands together, closed her small eyes and bowed her head. Ian stared at her, wondering what came next. After several seconds, she looked up at him expectantly. "Thank God for bacon 'n eggs."

Ian wasn't sure if this was a question, command or announcement. "What?" He asked for clarification.

She pointed at Ian for clarification. "Thank God for bacon 'n eggs."

"Me? Pray?" Ian was fully awake and aware at this point.

Emma didn't say a word in response as she bowed her head in wait.

Ian rubbed his forehead. He bent slightly to look into Emma's bowed face. The steam from the eggs between them blurred her features, but Ian could tell her eyes were still closed. Emma was in earnest.

"Listen, I'm not hungry this morning. You can tell whoever put you up to this that you did your job. You made breakfast of 'bacon n' eggs,' terms of the contract carried out and you're free to go." Ian watched her reaction. Emma didn't budge.

"You can go now. You made breakfast. All done."

"Emma wait."

"Wait for what?"

"Thank God for bacon 'n eggs."

"No, look, it's time for you to go. Whoever called you doesn't expect me to pray over some eggs with you. Besides, you should have knocked this morning and at least given me the courtesy of letting you in."

Emma's head was still bowed. Nothing was getting through to her. It finally occurred to Ian that whoever called this girl may have meant for it to be a practical joke, seeing as how she still hadn't moved and clearly couldn't converse.

"Oh my god, this is ludicrous!" Once again, Ian capitulated. He simply wanted all of this to end and Emma to disappear. With eyes wide open and a voice entirely lacking in enthusiasm, Ian spoke to the room, "Thanks for the bacon and eggs."

Emma didn't move.

"Amen," added Ian.

Emma's head popped up. She began distributing bacon and eggs to the two plates. She stabbed at the eggs, using her bacon as a shovel. Assessing the food on his plate, Ian began tasting it in turn. Determining it was edible, and seeing no alternatives before him, he began eating with more intensity, all the while watching Emma. For the first time in his life, he didn't know what to do.

"Do you live around here?" he asked between mouthfuls.

"Uh huh," Emma responded with a mouthful of eggs and a nod.

"Where exactly?"

"Around here."

"Where's 'around here'?"

"Yes."

"Oh my god, I've got Rainman in my kitchen!"

Getting nowhere in the verbal realm, Ian surveyed the girl's exterior. He could detect the intermingled odors of the piney outdoors, greasy bacon and slight body odor. Her clothes were dated and worn, but of excellent quality. Beneath her flannel button down, Ian detected three other layers of various patterns and degrees of wear. Her thick fingers were weather worn. Perhaps not weeks, but definitely days of dirt were wedged beneath her short jagged nails. Brown hair outlined her face in an old-fashioned pixie cut. Despite the grease and occasional flora, Ian could tell it was professionally cut. This caused Ian to come up short in his first assessment. The high-quality leather hiking boots were the right size for her feet, providing another mental stumbling block. Ian shook his head.

Just as he was putting the last bite of Emma eggs into his mouth, he heard a deep sigh emanate from behind the kitchen counter. Emma continued to stab and eat. Ian chalked the sounds up to expensive Scotch. Half the contents of his plate and all of Emma's were gone when Emma stood up. A few clatters ensued as she gathered her dishes. She stepped away from the table and revealed Ian's second hangover of the day.

In Emma's shadow stood the largest domesticated animal Ian had ever seen. He dropped his fork and jumped into a standing position on his chair.

"That Pax," said Emma.

"He doesn't need to pack anything. That's a monster!" Ian yelled from his vantage point.

Pax calmly sat and watched Emma busy herself. Ian cautiously made his way back into his chair. The closer to a sitting position Ian got, the more Pax's tail wagged. When Ian was finally seated, the dog made his way over to him with a smile and a wag.

"Pax like pet," offered Emma as she returned the half-and-half to the fridge.

Ian moved over to Emma's vacated chair, putting more distance between himself and the dog. The dog's black frame was massive, perhaps twice the size of the boxer he'd had growing up. The gentle sweep of his tail thrummed against the cupboards six feet away.

When Ian didn't return Pax's interest, Pax sat down, surveyed Ian again and gently dropped to the floor. There was no escape for Ian. The passage to the living room was blocked by the open refrigerator door. The passage to the mudroom was blocked by the horse Emma called Pax. He remained seated. Emma continued to clean up the breakfast remains.

"Um, you go ahead. I'll clean up," offered Ian.

She stood and stared at Ian for his inane remark.

"Emma clean breakfast," she insisted.

"No, really, you did all the work cooking, it's the least I can do," Ian pleaded. He couldn't remember the last time he sounded like that.

"Emma clean," and that was that.

Her hands moved slowly and carefully until all the ingredients were put away. Not as Ian would have (she left the shells in the egg carton and didn't place the red sugar bin with the clasp pointing outward). She picked up Ian's remaining breakfast on the silver-rimmed plaid plate and set it on the floor before Pax.

Ian shot back into a standing position on the chair, "Wait! No! You can't give him that plate. I had it custom made at Tiffany's! That's a fifty dollar plate!" He stood helpless and frantic on the chair.

With the clatter of the plate meeting the floor, a movement in the mudroom caught Ian's eye. Pax quietly stood up, glanced at Ian on the chair and hove to his breakfast. Emma placed her own plate on the floor as the mudroom movement took form.

"Give Rex turn, Pax," Emma informed her dog. She patted him gently on the head while another, larger version made his way to Emma's plate.

Ian hyperventilated. The throbbing in his head was augmented by a quickened pulse and loss of breath. He thought his eggs and coffee were going to come up.

Pax and Rex placidly peered at Emma. As she came across scraps, she fed them to each in turn. The plates made their way unscathed into the sink. Ian sat down with a sigh. She began to fill the sink with water and shot in a serving of soap.

"I'll wash," Ian piped up. " You've done all the cleaning. You can go now. And take your dogs with you. Besides, I've got a dishwasher for most of that." He looked hopefully at Emma and the dogs. No one moved.

"Emma almost done," she chirped. For the next ten minutes, Ian looked on as Emma washed, dried, and replaced every utensil and dish. She replaced the flour sack towel on the oven door and faced Ian.

"Emma done. Have good day." She donned the coat, hat, mittens, and scarf she had hung in the mudroom. With a parting wave, she and her dogs were out the mudroom door.

When the trio was gone, Ian stepped onto the porch, wrapping his arms around himself to fend off the chill. He took in her shape, smaller than her dogs', retreating into the woods north of the house. After the six-inch snowfall of the night before, she and her pack stood out in tremendous contrast. Clad in his pajamas and nothing more, Ian beat a hasty retreat back to the warmth of his house. He made sure the bolts were thrown on the front and mudroom doors before he picked up his phone and collapsed into his couch.

Chapter 4

MR. ROGER'S NEIGHBORHOOD

The sun was hitting the coffee table, urging Ian to abandon his nap. His feet hit the ground with a new resolve. After changing his clothes and smoothing his hair into place, he grabbed his phone and keys. First, he punched in a text to Kat. Perhaps she'd changed her mind. Perhaps she was experiencing deep regret and was simply waiting for an excuse to come back. He'd give her that excuse.

Pocketing his cell, he reached for his jacket and dressed for a drive. The Range Rover roared into life. He sat for a moment, deciding his course of action. With a plan, Ian threw the car into reverse and aimed down the drive.

Mount Laurel was a small, cheerful town. It had been the town of choice from which his search for land had radiated. Approving of its quaint Main Street and Myriad shops, Ian appreciated the setting and serenity it provided. He gladly acknowledged the educated and elite who summered there, somehow unanimously attracted to this singular town. Now, it was home.

Ian knew precisely one person by name in town: Russell Rogers, the real estate agent who had shown him the property he now owned. He pulled into a spot in front of a small white house with green shutters. Wedged between the candle shop and general store, the office maintained signage out front for passersby to see what was being offered on the real estate menu. *White House Real Estate* on the door ensured that one was purchasing acreage, not running for office.

A five nine mustachioed man stood up behind the solitary desk when Ian appeared. His bald spot was deftly hidden by a flatcap in deep tweed green. His bicolored brown saddle welts drew Ian's attention to the agent's other extreme.

"Mr. Campbell, welcome to Mount Laurel," the agent moved his mustache to make room for his yellowed teeth. Ian suspected a pipe was in permanent residence in the agent's right jacket pocket. It had not only left the lingering stains, but a warm aroma in the chill air of the office.

Ian was never one much for small talk. He eased into the eighties' answer to a King Louis chair and began his questioning.

"You've been here quite some time and know your way around. Where can one get a decent haircut in this town, Mr. Rogers?" He wondered if asking the man who lacked thatch was wise. Regardless, it was his only option at this juncture.

"Well, you know what they say when there are two barbers in town." Mr. Rogers warmed to the subject, and leaned back in his chair.

Ian thought there would be more, but realized the agent was waiting for a "who's there" from him. Ian reluctantly took the bait. "No, I'm afraid I'm unfamiliar with that one, Mr. Rogers. What do they say about two barbers in town?"

The agent took out his pipe, patted down the bowl contents and held it out for emphasis. "If one barber has a great haircut and a tidy shop, and the other barber has a terrible haircut and a messy shop which one should you engage?"

Rather than feed him lines all day, Ian cut to the chase, "So, which barber has the messy shop, Rogers? " He was hoping to make this visit as brief as possible.

Mr. Rogers gave a quiet harrumph and leaned forward in his chair. "That would be Simon over on Pine."

"How about southern food take-out? Any recommendations for a man who's lost his cook, but prefers to eat at home?"

"Seems to me it would be best to hire another cook, Mr. Campbell. A man needs consistent sustenance." Rogers lit his pipe feeling the upper hand in the exchange.

What was it with this place? He'd only been in the presence of two people in the last twelve hours and neither had been cooperative.

"Take-out, Mr. Rogers." He reiterated his point to get the requisite response. "Is there a restaurant which prepares decent evening meals which provides take-out?"

"Now that would be one and only one place: Sadie's Diner on Maple. She doesn't advertise her take-out option, but she'll pack it up for her repeat customers." He puffed out the last line with a cloud.

Ian got up to leave, "Thanks for your help, Mr. Rogers. I'll get the lay of the land soon enough, but I appreciate your help in the meantime."

With Ian's hand on the door pull, the agent made one last query, "Enjoying your place up there, Mr. Campbell? It sure has caught a few headlines, hasn't it? We're mighty proud of what you've added around here. Finding everything satisfactory and hunky-dory?" Rogers ran through his questions not looking for responses. He was doing the polite agent bit in case Ian had friends or family who might catch the mountain bug. That gave Ian the impetus to ask one more of his own. "Know anyone on my peak by the name of Emma?"

"Emma?" He spat the name rather than repeated it. "Can't say that I do. Sorry I couldn't be of help. Have a good day, Mr. Campbell," he swiveled a few degrees in his chair to let Ian know the conversation was over.

Ian stepped into the snap of the wind. Pine. He intended to find "Ol' Simon" on Pine as quickly as possible and get his hair into a more manageable state. Rather than get back in the Range Rover, he decided to get a little fresh air. Pine couldn't be more than a few short blocks away and he'd dressed for the weather. Exposure to the elements was what he needed to sharpen his mind and figure out how to get Kat back.

The clapper on the bell had broken years ago. Thus, it didn't tinkle to announce Ian's arrival, it did something more akin to a high pitched thud. The patrons and barber turned simultaneously. Before the barber could warn him, Ian rushed headlong into an exposed beam and stopped short. The locals sent out a collective, "oh" while Ian held his head and staggered over to the closest chair.

The mountain man next to him noted what everyone else was thinking, "New in town, eh?"

"My entry kind of gave it away, huh?" Ian squinted at the man.

"You can tell a local by the way they dodge the rafters," shared what must have been Ol' Simon. He sported a butcher's apron and forty shades of whiskers in relief. He cut hair reaching up at him from the lone salon chair in the room and talked to the waiting crowd. It made Ian think of barbering in the round. As Ian nursed his goose egg, he listened in rapt attention.

One would think the Mount Laurel commissioners had re-located their monthly meeting to Ol' Simon's. Inclement weather, national politics, gas prices, Syrian independence and the gamut of local interests were discussed and disagreed in the course of a haircut.

A patron didn't leave just because his hair was done. He simply traded places with someone else in the room. It didn't even seem to matter at what point someone entered the environs. If someone needed their hair cut pronto, they took the chair in front of Ol' Simon's scissors. If one wasn't in a hurry, they found their way there as their topic of interest arose.

Ian was pleasantly surprised by the savvy in the room. He had taken the old timers as uninformed. The fewer teeth a man had, Ian had assumed, the fewer pages of the paper he perused. Pete, who seemed to be the oldest and bragged the fewest teeth, managed to shatter any preconceived notions Ian had of these enigmatic mountain men. Pete had a remarkable working knowledge of any topic broached.

Ian was silently and unanimously voted onto the chair. He sat before the butcher's apron reasoning that no matter how bad the results looked, no one of any import would see him anyway.

"What's your preference, mister?" asked Ol' Simon. He tossed his scissors into a vessel of alcohol and yanked out another pair. Wiping the wetness off the blades, Simon held them close to Ian's scalp. He took in Ian's reflection.

"Can you just do a shorter version of what I've got now? Kind of trim it up?" coaxed Ian. With no point of reference for Simon's abilities, Ian decided not to try anything new.

"That can be done," agreed Ol' Simon, as he launched into a debate about the new permitting on the old general store.

Hair coiffed, Ian ducked with care as he left Ol' Simon's.

He took his seat behind the steering wheel of the Range Rover and started it up. While the engine warmed, Ian checked his texts again and wrote his fourteenth of the day to Kat. A precedent.

He called Shelly, too. When he'd stepped out of the courtroom and called Shelly the day Mr. Woodrow found his freedom, he had silently vowed he would never speak to her again. After all, that portion of his life was over, no need to check in with an assistant. This was one promise he'd have to break.

"Shelly? Yeah, hey. Oh, it's nice enough." He tried to frame his questions in such a way that Shelly would have no idea of his need, but be able to answer his questions informatively. "Say, has anyone been trying to get in touch with me? With the cell service I get here, I'm thinking I've missed a call or two." Not a lie, just not the truth.

"No? Good, that means I tidied up my accounts properly when I left. Thanks a bunch, Shelly." He was about to hang up and thought twice. "Oh, Shelly? If my service up here is faulty and you end up with some messages for me, would you call me personally to let me know? That way, I'm sure to get in touch with them. Great. Kat, oh, she's fine. Thanks, bye." Her question told him everything her answers had not.

As the sun was being edged out by the trees on a distant peak, Ian found Maple Street and secured a spot near the back door of Sadie's Diner. Hopefully, he could talk Sadie into letting him take her homemade food home.

Clinking of glasses and chatter of patrons surprised him. A sudden feeling overwhelmed his senses. He didn't recall feeling this way when he'd walked into a restaurant in Boston, NYC or even LA. In those venues, he'd only been energized or irritated. Had it been possible in his present milieu, this environment, these people, would have brought him a sense of cheer.

He made his way to the cash register and found it much easier than not to order flank steak and greens to go. He waited on the worn bench by the door. From there he had a good vantage point of the patrons who came and went. He found himself searching their faces as they chatted their way out of Sadie's.

"With extra dressing on the side, Mr. Campbell," smiled the cashier as she held a steaming white bag out to him. "Come again!"

Ian was sure he would if the food tasted as good as the service had been. He felt reluctant to leave, but shook it off before he could explore the feeling.

The drive home was exploratory rather than efficient. He took note of the Tasty Freeze, blinking "Tasty—eeze," as well as the clinic, library and produce stand, all on this route up the backside of his peak. These locales on route 129 were good to know. He passed a ski shop, craft store, and quilt shop, not bothering to look past the signage to the displayed wares beyond.

Winding his way up the mountain's southern exposure, he

meandered past second homes and rental cabins, and reached Uplands well after sunset. After disassembling in the mudroom, he made his way to the stove with his supper.

He extricated the flank steak leaving the salad in the box. While the salad chilled in the fridge, Ian heated up the flank steak on his Smeg Symphony. The silence chilled him. Before sitting down to Sadie's steak, he pulled the phone out of his pocket and muttered a muffled curse. Resigned, he pushed a few buttons and turned a few dials in the wall next to the fridge. Strains of Brahms accompanied him as he ate alone.

Chapter 5

BACON 'N EGGS

Ian woke with a start. The bed was as luxurious as the ads had claimed it to be. He couldn't remember the last time he'd slept a straight eight hours. Ian began peeling the covers back when he heard muffled movement below.

"Kat?" Ian jammed his feet into the slippers at the foot of his bed and raced down the stairs. He grabbed the last spindle of the bannister to slow himself down. There at the foot of the stairs were the colossal canines of yesterday. Standing on the penultimate step, he inquired, "Um, Irma, er, Emma? Are you there? Is that you?" Had he anticipated anyone else, he would never have asked such insipid questions.

Emma peeked around the open fridge door. "Emma cook breakfast." She buried her head behind the open door again.

"No, no, Emma *don't* cook breakfast." Ian gingerly made his way through the maze of dog to the kitchen. "Emma, this isn't your house. You don't live here. You don't cook breakfast here." Ian insisted as she made her way to and from the stove.

"Emma make bacon 'n eggs," she reminded him as she broke the eggs in the pan.

"Can't Emma make bacon and eggs at *her* house?" asked Ian.

"Emma make eggs here. For you." She pointed at Ian for

clarification.

"No, I don't need breakfast! I don't want breakfast! I'm good with a cup of coffee. You can go now."

"Emma get coffee, too."

"No, *I'll* get coffee while *you* go home." Ian stood in front of the coffee maker barring Emma's way. She walked around him to the red sugar bin and placed it on the table. She edged past him to the refrigerator to collect the half-and-half. She opened the freezer to withdraw the coffee grounds. Never hastening, but always purposeful, she pushed the eggs around the pan before they burned.

Ian stood resolute. Preparing a plate of the remaining bacon and setting it in the microwave, she pushed button after button to no avail.

"What buttons make 'wave go?" asked Emma.

"Don't you remember from yesterday?" he accused Emma. "What am I talking about?" he said to himself. "You aren't supposed to be cooking my breakfast. There's some kind of mistake!"

"No steak. Emma make bacon 'n eggs." She stared at the microwave and began pushing buttons again.

Ian shoved her away from the microwave. "You're going to break it if you keep that up!" he snapped. He pushed the requisite three buttons only to find Emma at the abandoned coffee maker.

Ian threw up his hands in defeat and sat down. "How do you even get in? Are you Houdini's granddaughter or something?"

"No. Name Emma," she clarified as she placed eggs on a plate and set them on the table. The microwave beeped its readiness. Emma plated the bacon, setting it before Ian. He was surprised that somehow she had also managed to make coffee and had everything before him in ten minutes flat. That was some kind of miracle, Ian was sure.

Resigned to his situation, he ate. Between sips of coffee he practiced his best examination techniques on Emma. He got repeats of past answers.

"I know, I know, 'Emma makes bacon 'n eggs.' What I want to know is how you're getting into my house," he snapped.

"Emma use key," she revealed.

"Key? How in the world did you get a key?" Ian was incredulous. There were only three keys to Uplands. He and Kat each had one and the third was in the custody of the maid.

"Left Emma key."

"What? I didn't leave a key anywhere." Ian was speaking at a higher pitch with every answer. He willed himself to calm down. In spite of the caliber client he'd had through the years, he'd never been so dogged in a line of questioning as he now was by this simple woman.

Dishes clattered as Emma began clearing the table. Ian tried to grab his plate before she did, but hadn't remembered in time. The mammoths entered the kitchen, and Ian retreated to Emma's vacated seat.

"Look, Irma, er Emma, could you, *please*, not feed the dogs on my china?" Ian envisioned one huge pooch paw on the edge of the small plate breaking it into pieces.

"Pax and Rex like bacon 'n eggs," she answered as she caressed their ears.

"Then just ..." Ian waved his hands above his head at loss for words, "dump the food on the floor or something!" He forced himself to calm down. "I can always mop up later."

"Emma wash dishes." She placed the dishes in the sink and started the water running.

"No, no, I'll do that. You've done enough today. Just go."

"Emma clean up after." Her resolute reaction gave Ian no choice but to either watch or help. Eventually, the food found its way into the fridge and the dishes were washed and dried while Ian sipped and sulked.

"Emma, can you show me your key?" Ian asked as she put the last of the dried dishes away. Gently, Emma drew a key out of her pocket. Attached to it was a keychain bearing the Laurel Mountain city crest. It was the maid's key.

"Where did you find that key, Emma?" Ian was calmer

now, trying to piece together the inscrutable mystery.

"Emma's mat," and she turned to look at the mudroom door. He thought he could piece some things together if Emma could continue to answer with new words; so far, so good. This was the most progress he'd made all day. The dogs sensed Emma's readiness and walked to the door.

"Bye bye," she said as she put on her hat, gloves and coat. She struggled to button the small buttons with her large fingers. When everything was in place, she put her hand on the knob to let herself and her entourage out. Ian stood with his hand out, robe tie trailing on the floor, hair a mess, face set with a determined look.

"Emma, give me your key. It's mine really. I made the key and bought the key and it's my house it goes to." Ian was hopeful the simple logic would rule the moment.

"Emma's key," she declared and stepped out into the cold. He followed her out, and shouted into the air after her, "Keep the key, but don't come back unless you're going to knock!" Ian's Hail Mary pass had failed.

Two weeks later, Ian had sent one hundred twenty-seven texts, made forty two phone calls and dialed every relative or friend Kat had. Ian didn't want to reveal the situation. After all, how did one go about saying he'd misplaced his wife? How was he to put it that she hadn't come with him to live out the dream? How did one reveal their hand without hinting at their heart? He used subtle questions and gave little information. Everyone he called, including Kat's family, thought she was at Uplands. He had no more ideas, no leads.

Hot cocoa swirled in his mug as he faced the fire and fancied new strategies. As he pulled Kat's letter from his wallet, it tore. He pieced it together and read it again, looking for any clues he may have missed the first fifty times he'd read it. Nothing new appeared to him. No new hints leapt out at him as to where she was. No clarity came to him as to why she'd done it. He carefully refolded the letter and tucked it into his wallet, then slammed his fist against the couch cushion.

"Empty? No one? Has the maid been there?" His obvious questions to the doorman were subtle ways of finding out whether Kat had been hiding out at home. "But you haven't seen anyone else coming or going? No, no, I suppose my remote software must not be functioning properly. If you could get the manager to check my thermostat for me, I'd appreciate it. It's Alfred, right? Thank you, Alfred. Let me know if you see anyone suspicious or if anything changes. Oh, and give *me* a call not Mrs. Campbell. I don't want to unduly alarm her." Although the malfunctioning thermostat ploy had kept Alfred off the scent, it had only led to more dead ends for Ian. Kat hadn't been home.

He trained his thoughts on another front. It had been two weeks of daily visits and all he'd gotten out of Emma were the same six statements. Of this Ian was certain:

Emma felt a sense of ownership of the key. Short of assault and battery, there was no getting the key from her.

Emma was going to make breakfast for him whether he liked it or not.

Emma was going to make bacon and eggs for breakfast, no matter what.

Emma arrived some time between 6:00 and 6:30. (Ian fixed the time based on when she woke him with her entrance or scurrying about.)

Breakfast was on the table at 7:00.

He'd pieced enough together to know that the day before he'd arrived, the maid had left her key under the mat rather than take it with her when she dropped off his groceries. For whatever mysterious reason, Emma had come along, looked under the mudroom mat, "Emma's mat" she had called it, and procured the key for herself. Why she looked under that mat

Ian had no idea. Why she came in every morning and made the two of them bacon and eggs and sat with Ian to eat it was the bigger mystery, yet to be solved.

In all the years of solving mysteries and revealing them to juries, he'd never been so flummoxed. He'd never come up against anything as resolute or enigmatic as Emma.

Instead of living the dream, Ian was living the paradox: he couldn't find his wife, and he couldn't rid himself of this stranger.

Emma stood staring into the refrigerator. Ian silently peeked over the back of the couch. He had purposely slept there to witness the results of his latest attempt to thwart her. In hopes of a longed-for victory, Ian had done his own grocery shopping, omitting bacon and eggs.

Emma was clearly outfoxed. She closed the refrigerator door and took the closest chair in the breakfast nook. With hands clasped in her lap and a far away look in her eye, she considered. The dogs collapsed in a contented heap at the bottom of the stairs. Ian noticed they placed themselves in the most trafficked place in the house. It was as irritating as it was inconvenient.

Ian took this opportunity to complete the *coup de gras*. He stretched and yawned his way into the kitchen, feigning a wakening. She hadn't stirred, so he pushed the issue.

"Good morning, Emma," he greeted. It was the most sincere welcome he'd ever managed. "Can I get you some coffee?" He came from around the couch and began depositing a filter in the coffee maker.

"No bacon 'n eggs?" she asked.

"I'm afraid not. No bacon or eggs. I have stricken them from my diet and will not have them in my refrigerator from now on." He continued going through the motions of coffee for two. There was a spring in his step, buoyed by the idea that this would be his last morning with Emma. She stared into the space between the refrigerator and the cupboard.

"No bacon?" she piecemealed.

"Nope. None."

"No eggs?"

"No, not one."

Emma got up, replaced her recently released clothing and left the house, dogs in tow. Ian watched her head south. He danced a brief victory jig, flipped off the coffee maker, and leapt back on to the couch to finish his repose. These early mornings had caught up to him.

An hour later, Ian breathed in the strong odor of bacon frying. He unconsciously took in the gentle sizzle of eggs in heated butter. Jerking awake, he stared over the back of the couch.

Emma was back. The coffee maker was sputtering and spewing a fresh brew. Everything was back in its place of the last two weeks – except Ian. He groaned and fell back into his blankets. Groundhog Day. He was stuck on the same day waking to Emma cooking bacon and eggs for the rest of his life; his perfectly planned, retired life.

"Unbelievable," he spoke to the ceiling, "Where did this girl find bacon AND eggs before dawn on a Saturday morning?" He threw back the covers, planted his feet on the floor and raked his fingers through his hair. Making his way to the kitchen, he avoided the sprawled Pax and Rex with an acquired alacrity.

"Emma cook bacon 'n eggs," she announced to Ian as he entered the kitchen.

"Where in the world did you get them?" he inquired over her shoulder. His incredulity was coupled with dismay.

"Emma got bacon 'n eggs."

"Yes, I see that. What I want to know," Ian seated himself with a sigh, "is *where* you got them."

She looked askance at Ian. "Bacon 'n eggs come from farm," she informed him. With his face in his hands, Ian muffled a sob.

BETSY BOYD LESLIE

Chapter 6

TRIAGE

With the recent failure behind him, and a full stomach of bacon and eggs, Ian felt a touch of anticipation as he considered a possible victory, on another front, before noon. A new thought had struck him last night as he was drifting off to sleep. He would contact the cell phone company and track Kat's phone. He'd never been the stalker type, so he wasn't sure how that was done. Finding clients via this method had been Shelly's purview, not his. He placed a call to his cell phone service provider.

"I'm sorry, I missed it. What did you say your name was?" he asked into his phone. "Samantha? Samantha, my wife has set her phone down where we can't find it. It's probably comfortably tucked into our couch or underneath a car seat somewhere. With dead batteries, it's kind of hard to call it. I understand you have some sort of GPS device for locating phones. Would you, please, work your magic and find it for us?" He forced a chuckle. "Sure, I'll hold." Ian was always careful to be honest. He hadn't told a lie, he just hadn't defined his terms.

"Great, here's the number." For the first time since he'd read Kat's note, he felt hopeful. He tapped his finger against his desk while he waited. After taking in the framed efforts of the masters on the opposite wall, his eyes regained focus as he listened to Samantha.

"I have to come in to the office? Why can't you just give me the information over the phone?"

Ian listened, the victorious smile quickly fading into a frown of failure.

"'Office policy?' 'Security features?'" He felt like a bad witness repeating all of the lawyer's questions.

"But I can give you some secret code word and you'll know it's me, the account holder. You know, the street I grew up on, my first dog, where I went to high school. "

Ian listened.

"What special security features?" A light suddenly dawned.

"In person?" Ian recalled getting the maximum security features on his phone in the event his phone was stolen or misplaced. The idea was that in his line of work, it wouldn't do for anyone other than himself to have access to the information contained in his phone. *He* didn't even like having access to the information contained in his phone. Not with some of the clientele he'd had over the years. He simply hadn't counted on *this* event – losing the wife who carried the phone.

He gritted his teeth and let out a breath.

"Where is your closest branch?" He found himself asking. He gave her his address and waited.

"But isn't that two hours from here? Are you sure you entered the correct zip code? Would you, please, double check?"

Ian waited.

"You are *absolutely certain* that is your closest branch?" Suddenly Waltham's Peak didn't sound like the perfect location any more.

"Thank you, Samantha. Yeah, you too." He hung up and stared into the space between the refrigerator and the cupboards.

"What? What do you mean the information isn't accurate?" Ian paused to take in the associate's information. He couldn't believe his ears. He had just driven over two hours one-way to get helpful information, not this. Not a dead end. Not Jaime's accented soliloquy regarding the phone's anticlimactic usage.

"So what you're telling me is that since she hasn't used it in two and a half weeks, and the plan ran out last week and hasn't been renewed, that the only information you can give me is that the phone was last used in Boston at our home address on November 10th?" That was the day he'd left town.

Within five minutes of reaching his destination, he was utterly and completely out of questions, ideas and hope. He climbed back into the Range Rover, gassed up and raced back to Uplands.

Two hours gave him plenty of time to think - and stew. Gravel was shoved into his off road tread as he slammed on the brakes outside his front door. Taking the stairs two at a time, he threw open the front door and raced up the indoor flight. Furiously, he jerked open drawers and yanked out files until he found what he was looking for: the phone bill. He was going to look up one more thing he'd forgotten to ask the clerk.

Why hadn't he noticed earlier? Both he and Kat's names were on the plan. She could make changes at will without his signature. Or drop the plan. He dialed the penthouse manager, a number he'd added to his list when he called last week about the "alarm."

"Would you have the doorman, Alfred, yeah that's the name, phone me, please. He's been helping me with the alarm malfunction in my flat. Thank you."

Within minutes his phone buzzed.

"Hello, Alfred? This is Ian Campbell. I phoned you last week about the thermostat malfunction. Would you do me a favor? Thanks, good. I think Mrs. Campbell left her phone in the penthouse. Could you take a quick look and let me know if you find it? The batteries are dead by now, so I can't help you with a ring. Good, thanks. Call me when you've got some results."

He picked up the same pencil he'd tapped yesterday and began tapping it against his specially ordered desk. Although he didn't intend to "work" at the desk, he had intended to be productive. Research, reading, and some writing had all been part of his retirement plan.

Alfred's voice following his cell ringing brought him back to the work before him.

"It was? Where did you find it? On the desk? Sitting there with some keys? What keys do they appear to be? Could you rattle off for me the inscriptions on them?" He waited again and tapped. "Ford, Schlade, and Baldwin? The keychain has a brass Mickey Mouse on it, doesn't it? Yeah, that's what I thought. Thanks, Alfred. No wonder she couldn't find her keys. You've done us a huge favor."

So Kat had turned off the phone and left it in the penthouse. All this time, including the night he left when he texted Kat from the penthouse, it had been right there within striking distance, not on Kat. What's more, she had left *all* her keys. The three the doorman had rattled off included her car, the penthouse and Uplands. A minimalist, those were the only keys Kat ever had on her fob. She had meant it when she said she was taking nothing. For the first time since he'd read her note, Ian wept.

The sign read "24 Hour Clinic," but here he sat in the dark.

"I'm sorry, Mr. um," there was a brief delay as the nurse looked down at the chart for his name, "Campbell. But we shut off the lights after 9:00 in all the empty rooms to save on energy."

"That's fine, nurse, um," it occurred to him how easy it was to be a jerk. He knew perfectly well her name was Patty. It was sewn into her scrubs pocket. He peered at it now, giving it a squint, "… Patty, I didn't need to watch myself bleed to death anyway."

As tired as she appeared, she took his sarcasm in stride.

"Dr. Preston will be right with you. The patient before you turned out to be a bit more complicated a matter than we thought it would be." She left through the same door and disappeared, presumably to help Dr. Preston with the needy patient. Earlier, she had taken only a cursory look at Ian's bloodstained UVA shirt and the mutilated flesh beneath. Surely, thought Ian, this wasn't how triage was meant to be implemented.

Ian woke with a start when another scrub-clad woman, curly hair askew, stood before him, hands on hips, lips mouthing his name. Words began to form in Ian's head. They finally burst into reality.

"Mr. Campbell, are you ready to be seen now?"

After an hour in the abandoned waiting room, Ian had given up hope of remaining awake. He wasn't happy about his wait, the throbbing in his finger, or the new crick in his neck. Now he'd need an x-ray of his spine, too.

"Sure, if Dr. Preston thinks he can fit me in tonight," he snapped. The woman turned to lead him down the hall, stopped short with the retort, and pointed to a room. Patty followed them into Room 1 bearing a tray laden with a medical sewing kit.

"You get the guest of honor seat, Mr. Campbell," she gestured to the examination table. The crinkle of the paper and the brightness of the lights poked Ian awake.

"Now tell me what we've got here." The curly haired woman turned the faucets to the mini sink and began vigorously scrubbing her hands and forearms. Ian watched her dry off and wondered why she didn't collect her fallen curls.

"As I mentioned to Patty here," Ian verbally stabbed at them both for having to tell the story twice, "I was chopping wood and the axe slipped. I think I severed a nerve or artery or something, because the thing hurts like hell and bleeds like a faucet. I'm probably in some kind of shock now with all the blood loss and time lapse, so be sure to check my vitals."

The two women exchanged glances. With gloved hands,

Patty began peeling back the blood-encrusted shirt wrapped around Ian's thumb. The other woman looked on while Patty cleaned and bathed the finger with gauze pads and alcohol. Ian sucked in his breath and looked away from his finger into the eyes of the curly-haired woman. A smile broke out on her face.

"And what do you find so amusing?" he snapped.

"Fingers don't burn nearly as well or as long as cordwood, Mr. Campbell." She snapped on some latex gloves, pulled a rolling chair over with her foot and sat down to inspect his wound. She held his hand, carefully turning and peering at the damage without touching the wound.

"Well, Mr. Campbell, there's good news and there's bad news. Which would you like first?" She stared up at him waiting for a response. Patty stood at the ready, sewing kit in hand.

"Today's been a tough day, lady. Could you and Patty just get Dr. Preston in here and get this show on the road?" Ian thought back to his failed plans of this morning to extricate Emma from his life once and for all. He thought back to the dead end he'd run into in Hickory. He thought back to the phone and keys left on the desk in Boston. He thought back to the flat tire he'd gotten on his way back from the blasted office. He thought back to the empty house, unmade supper, and dwindling wood supply which had landed him here. He wasn't in the mood for games.

"Well, Mr. Campbell, the good news is that we can have you sewn up in about ten minutes and send you on your way." She released his mangled hand and began threading a threateningly large needle as she continued. "The bad news is that *I'm* the doctor."

Chapter 7

WALTHAM'S GIRL

Although Ian didn't get home until almost midnight, he had the mental clarity to develop a new plan. He had to. He was going to have another visit from the short order cook in less than six hours. Before he took the stairs up to bed, he set in motion the plans for the morning. Yes, he'd had a terrible day, but he was beginning to look forward to the promise of the morrow.

He showered carefully, following the doctor's instructions not to moisten or aggravate the stitched area. Aggravated? Too late, he already was. A few aspirins later and Ian was sound asleep.

For the first time, he awoke to the clarion call of "breakfas'!" With the thick slurring of r and the altogether missing t, there was no mistaking it was Emma. Slippered and robed, Ian appeared in the kitchen. He was smiling in anticipation of his victory.

In spite of the fact that he had unplugged every appliance but the fridge, Emma had managed to improvise. Instead of microwaved bacon, she had cooked it in a pan. The grease

49

splatters all over his backsplash and stovetop told that story. Instead of coffee, Emma had filled his usual cup with hot tea, complete with the usual cream and sugar. Evidently, unless the refrigerator and range were removed, Emma would not be thwarted.

Ian stepped over the monoliths and took his usual seat. Morose as he was, he found himself eating every last morsel of Emma's "bacon 'n eggs."

At the thudding of the bell, Ian deftly ducked as he entered Ol' Simon's shop. Half a dozen pairs of eyes settled on him. The bandage on his thumb was hard to miss.

"Looks like you're running into more than just rafters, mister." Ian considered the jibe, but chose to ignore it. He was on a mission.

"A free haircut for anyone who can tell me who Emma near Waltham's Peak is," Ian announced to the room. Half a dozen pairs of eyes settled on him.

"That'll be six free haircuts for us and a hole in your wallet, mister," said Pete indicating the others in the room with a nod.

"You mean *all* of you know who Emma is?" Ian was flabbergasted. He had assumed that a mystery to him, meant a mystery to everyone.

"Of course. She's Old Man Waltham's girl," offered the mountain man on his right.

"Where's he?" asked Ian.

"Heaven we presume,' but we don't rightly know beyond the Myrtle Hill Cemetery," answered the florist on his lunch hour.

"With whom does she live?" pressed Ian.

"Nobody."

"Are we talking about the same Emma? Two huge dogs and somewhere on the autism spectrum?"

"Yep, that there's Emma Waltham. She lives on the backside of Waltham Peak all by herself and them dogs," added a voice from the left.

"You mean Waltham Peak off 129?"

"You're quick, mister," encouraged the mountain man. A good-natured chuckle circled the room.

"I'm assuming," Ian shot the encourager a look," that the Walthams owned the land on Waltham's Peak. How much did they own and when did they sell it?" continued Ian.

At this, Pete felt obliged to respond, "What do you go by, mister? It might be a little easier to address you if I've got a name to work with."

"Campbell. Ian Campbell."

Pete's features took on a knowing smile as he told the tale. He leaned back in his worn chair and rested his elbows on its arms. Ian thought this was the same chair he'd seen this same man in the last time he'd visited Ol' Simon. Had he stirred from there since? Ian doubted as much. For that matter, Simon seemed to not have gotten very far. Clean butcher's apron aside, he hadn't budged since Ian saw him last.

Pete continued. "The Walthams were millionaires come down from up north. Old Man Waltham made his money in the railroads buildin' 'em and runnin' 'em. He and the family started winterin' here when his health turned. They bought five hundred acres of what used to be the town's namesake: Laurel Mountain. They chose it for the vantage point and leveled off area for their fancy home. They had a passel of kids, four if I recollect, mostly growed, when they moved in. In Mrs. Waltham's later years, they had another baby. That there Emma." Pete leaned forward and spit with tremendous accuracy into the waiting Folger's can.

"About the time Emma was turnin' teens, Mrs. Waltham turned sick and passed away. Old Man Waltham and Emma lived in his big old place year round for the next eight or nine years. When Old Man Waltham saw the writin' on the wall, he built a little place for Emma a ways from the house. He knew she wouldn't be able to care for herself and that old ramblin', house, so he got ready. He taught Emma how to live on her own and got Judge Lewis to write up a trust for her."

The only sounds in the room were Simon's scissors and the

heat wheezing through the radiator. Everyone else seemed familiar with this story. Everyone but Ian whose house key she coveted.

Pete carried on. "For some reason, Emma took to life on her own. Waltham got her a couple behemoths as pups to protect her. Everyone in town knows Emma and them pups. Simon here cuts her hair once a month. Sadie saves scraps for the pups. The mayor, whose family was good friends with the Walthams, makes sure she's got clothes and such. The trust ran out a couple years back when the stock market crashed. Emma don't know, but she don't need to, cause we all see to her. Besides, there's only so much help Emma will take."

Ian sat stunned. All the answers to his questions had been sitting right here all this time.

"And that's where you come in, Mr. Campbell."

Ian frowned in confusion at Pete, "Me?"

"If I'm as quick as you are, I'd say you're the Mr. Campbell who up and bought all of Old Man Waltham's Peak last year. You tore down what was left of Waltham's place and put up somethin' mighty grand." He let out a low whistle to confirm the beauty of Uplands. The barbershop audience silently assented.

"Sounds to me, Mr. Campbell," chimed in another local, "you bought more than you bargained for."

"Thanks for the information," remarked Ian. He stood up, carefully fetched his wallet from inside his bomber jacket and handed Simon a wad of cash. "That should cover cut and tip for six, Simon." Simon buried the wad somewhere in his folds of butcher's apron.

"And here's a tip for you, Mr. Campbell," offered Pete, "don't go harmin' our Emma or the town will square with you."

Ian looked him square in the eye, "I've got some settlin' of my own to do, Pete. Emma's certainly a fly in the ointment, but I don't wish her any harm." He tucked his wallet away, ducked with precision and closed the jangling door behind him.

The door flew open and Kat rushed to the couch, leaping on the cushion next to Ian where he sat studying. "Your favorite, Honey! Sweet and sour chicken from Mai Ping's, and it's a beautiful night." She began pulling on him.

"Kat, I can't. I've got to study." He pulled his arm away from her grasp.

"Ian, you've got the highest average in the class by twelve points and you've already won the clerkship. One serving of Mai Ping and a few constellations aren't going to keep you from a Senate seat someday. Now come on." Kat grabbed his foot and tugged.

Like an old camel, Ian slowly removed his feet from the ottoman, found his shoes and jacket and grabbed his keys.

Kat put the last of the chicken in Ian's mouth with a quick flourish of chopsticks. She licked them off and packed up the trash, setting it beneath their park bench. Pulling the sleeves to her sweater down over her hands, she leaned against Ian and drew her legs up against her chest. Enamored with the stars, Kat said, "I told you it was beautiful out."

"It's too cold for beauty." Ian zipped up his jacket and held her to him.

"With an astronomical show like this? Are you kidding? Look, there's Orion clear as a bell, and ..."

Ian grabbed her hand as she reached up to point at her find. Kat smiled at him as he drew her hand toward his face. He surveyed her sleeve. "Kat, haven't I asked you not to wear this sweater anymore?" Kat's smile began fading. "It's not asking much, Kat. Why can't you bring yourself to do the smallest things for me?"

BETSY BOYD LESLIE

Chapter 8

MOUNTAIN TERMS

The door slammed open as Ian pushed his way into the White House Real Estate Office. "You lied to me, Rogers!" His fist landed on the desk splashing business cards onto the floor.

"What in heaven's name are you talking about, Mr. Campbell?" The agent grabbed his pipe off the desk for fear it would suffer a similar fate.

"For starters, telling me you didn't know anyone named Emma up near my place. Secondly, you sold me a bill of goods when you let me sign my name to a place that someone else was living on." The crescendo in Ian's voice grew until the word "on" was a shout. "I oughta sue you, Rogers!"

"Whoa, now, Mr. Campbell." Rogers wheeled back in his chair and wiped his face with a handkerchief. "Let me be reeeaaal clear now." He spread his hands out in the universal symbol for "slow down."

I *don't* know someone by the name of Emma on your piece of land. I know *of* her and a tad *about* her, but until this very moment I could not have told you her name. Furthermore," he regained his position in the chair, "according to the terms of the North Carolina realtor contract, it is my duty to, and I quote, 'reveal known damages, levies, encumbrances, or

55

appendages to said land.'

If you recall, I drove you and the misses around Waltham's Peak and pointed out all the outbuildings. One of those buildings I presume you believe this Emma lives in. I cannot confirm or deny that. I followed the terms of my contract and *revealed* those appendages to you." Rogers placed extra stress on "revealed" as if the emphasis itself revealed something to Ian. "What you chose to do with that knowledge, ignore it or increase it, was entirely up to you."

Ian wanted to spit. "You have evaded the truth, Rogers. You feigned ignorance and turned blind eyes to avoid responsibility. I will see you in court. You deliberately mislead me, Rogers!" He turned to go.

"Mr. Campbell," Rogers leaned forward and took on his best close-the-deal stance, "before you rush off in a huff to do just that, listen to me." Ian wasn't inclined to do so, but this new tack and tone intrigued him. He faced Rogers as his fingers squeezed the doorknob.

Rogers leaned forward, "In the real estate business, we do everything we can to represent our seller well *and* provide the buyer with exactly what he's looking for. When do you, as an attorney of law, ever have the burden in your line of work to meet the demands of both sides?"

Although Ian wasn't buying the excuse, he considered it an interesting argument.

"I did the best I could for both parties while playing by the book. Besides, what a judge will look at here are mountain terms. Do you have any idea how challenging it is to find squatters in fifty, twenty, even ten acres of heavily wooded land in the mountains? Even when you're looking for them? People, buildings, you name it, are simply needles in haystacks up here. Now, I mean no offense to you and your Emma, but this sort of thing happens up here all the time. A judge will rule every day of the week that I followed the terms, the *mountain terms*, of that contract. Don't waste your good time and money, Mr. Campbell."

Ian sat at the Tasty--eeze nursing a grudge and a latte. What was he thinking? What would he sue for, anyway? He needed to get the girl evicted and into a home. She had no business living alone, especially on *his* land. Clearly, the next step was to find this home of hers and begin the paperwork. Although he'd never completed a transaction like this for a client, he knew they were sticky at best and lengthy at worst. He swished back the remaining latte with his good hand and slammed the empty cup into the trash on his way out the door.

Emma usually arrived around 6:30 and had breakfast on the table by 7:00 a.m., depending on weather conditions. He would set his alarm for 6:00 and watch to see from which direction she came. He sat on his bed and adjusted the numbers on his bedside alarm. To ensure that his plan wasn't foiled, he did the same for his cell and left it next to the clock.

He padded down the stairs in his favorite Merino wool socks to the dining room. Floor to ceiling shelves on the exterior wall encased windows and framed the room. The built in bookshelves gave the illusion of holding up the stairs. Lighted cabinetry for china and collectibles revealed an educated assortment of valuable vases and first editions. Punctuated by a bust here and a framed print there, his library had been carefully shelved and organized for use and aesthetics.

Ian leaned against a dining chair and took in the collected contents. Dickens, Shakespeare, Doyle, Wodehouse, Jeremy, Sayers, and a plethora of other favorites, stared back at him. A wheeled ladder could be employed along the entire east wall to reach the books near the floor above.

Aside from his cell phone and a laptop, which remained in the sitting area upstairs, there were no other electronics in the house. Ian didn't believe in screens. Newspapers, periodicals, books, in short, anything in print, was what Ian preferred for whiling away his hours. Information was his friend.

He disliked the fits and starts of texts. They felt like advertisements to him; all tease and no tell. What he preferred was a long piece of prose. Just as good was a study, a committee report, a thesis which revealed a plethora of data with a point. Plots and points were the purpose of life, after all. If there was no point, well, then there was no point.

He selected a Sayers he'd read numerous times. What he needed now, he reasoned, was a well-written mystery to which he already knew the outcome. Real mysteries were highly overrated. With the book hugged against his hip, he poured himself a glass of wine and slid into his favorite reading chair. Shortly, he was consumed by the large leather chair and the antics of Lord Wimsey.

Chapter 9

OUTCASTS AND OUTBUILDINGS

"Morning," said Emma as she peered at Ian. Ian yawned, taking in the smiling face of Emma and the panting Rex and Pax peering at him. Immediately, he was wide awake.

"Damn," he offered in frustration. "What time is it?" He looked at the grandfather clock ticking among the books.

"Time for breakfas'," supplied Emma.

After Emma and her entourage left the house, Ian quickly drew on his warmest jacket, and hustled out the door with his binoculars. He noted that her footsteps were easily detected in the latest snow, so the fact that he'd missed his alarm hadn't set him back as much as he thought. His plans for the day might work after all. Retracing his steps to the house, he ran upstairs and dressed for a day outdoors. With temperatures in the twenties, he chose his layers carefully. He grabbed some energy bars, bottled water, and a few sundry articles, stuffed them in a backpack, locked the door behind him, and followed Emma's retreating footprints into the woods. Not knowing where Emma lived, he reckoned the round trip could take the greater part of the morning. As such, he paced himself. He'd been a cross-country runner in high school, so he knew a tad about preserving oneself for the homestretch.

Two miles was what Ian figured he'd trod by the time Emma's prints reached something akin to a home. He surveyed it from a distance, not wanting to frighten her, her dogs, or even himself. He had no idea what he would find.

Old Man Waltham was no dummy. The structure looked sound and snug. Four, perhaps five hundred square feet, were enclosed by thick log walls creating a rectangular footprint. After all the research Ian had done on weather efficiency, he could guess as to what lay behind the lumber. The panes were twice as deep as a typical home, allowing for greater amounts of fiberglass, straw, or whatever the insulation of choice happened to be. The windows were the most efficient windows on the market, allowing for ventilation in the cool months, warmth in the cold months. One chimney thrust up out of the snow-covered aluminum roof. No smoke appeared. No lights were on in the house.

Ian had approached from the south, and the home, Ian could safely call it that now, faced east. Sensing no one was about, he walked up to the front door. He knocked three times. He waited. Given the size of the home, if anyone was inside they would have answered the door by now. He stepped to the side of the door and looked in one of the windows. There were curtains drawn to the side, framing his view of the interior. What he saw was quaint. A made bed was tucked into the southwest corner of the two-room dwelling, at the base of which was a large pad, presumably for one or both of the dogs.

The northwest corner was a small walled-off room, clearly the bathroom. A kitchen was placed near the bath to most effectively utilize plumbing. She had a gas stove. No wonder Emma could make "bacon 'n eggs" on Ian's Smeg. A fridge, not dorm-sized, but not family-sized, stood in the opposite corner from the bathroom, flanking the counters and sink. The cupboards, counters and appliances were all the best brands, highest quality. The cottage design and decorations were comfortable and complementary. Pete was right; Old Man Waltham set her up well.

Taking in all he could from that vantage point, Ian made his way over to the window closest to Emma's bed. From this perspective he could see the back of the front door. To welcome her home, a large oval braided rug rested just inside the door. It was encircled by a couch, two plush armchairs, and reading lamps. Centering it all was a thick, rustic coffee table.

Not a thing was out of place. Emma took as good care of her own place as she did cleaning up after breakfast every morning at Uplands. The Walthams must have exercised tremendous patience throughout the years to have taught her so well. Few lawyers Ian knew could keep a place this tidy and take care of themselves.

Thankfully, the dogs had recently played in the snow Ian had traversed, creating havoc in the snow with his own prints. He didn't want Emma coming home to strange footsteps around her place. Ousting her was one thing, frightening her another.

Ian seated himself on a stump to fish his water bottle out of the backpack. He took in the cottage, considering its occupants. Carefully constructed and well maintained, it was definitely an asset on his acreage. An asset he'd seen from a moving vehicle more than a year ago. At the time, with the cavalier attitude of Rogers and his own excitement at his find, Ian hadn't given any of the "outbuildings" a second thought. He assumed any information of importance regarding his purchase would be made known to him. Courtesy call aside, that was the way real estate transactions were to be made. None of this "buyer beware" business; that was for used car salesmen and black market buyers. Any way he looked at it, he had been bested by Russell Rogers.

He screwed the cap back on his bottle and swung the pack back into place. It would all work out in the end. By his reckoning, his property value had just increased by several thousands of dollars. All at the expense of room service for the past several weeks.

Glancing at his watch and the sun, Ian considered what to do next. It was still early afternoon. He had nothing else to do but work on a puzzle he'd started the night before. He laughed out loud as the irony struck him: another puzzle.

He found Emma's tracks leading off to the west and decided to follow them. Anything he could uncover about her would be helpful. Especially if it helped him fill out eviction paperwork or qualify her for placement in a state institution. After all, he'd feel better, and the town would be more understanding if he provided Emma with some options when he evicted her.

Before setting off, he withdrew his compass and cell phone from the pack. He took his bearings with the compass and wrote down the GPS coordinates illuminated on his cell. He wanted to be able to return without a set of prints to follow.

An hour later, two more structures hove into view. Both of them emitted a grey curl of smoke. Ian found a tree large enough to hide himself and his backpack behind. He knelt down in the snow and rummaged through his backpack. After a few more swigs of water, he grabbed his binoculars and set about adjusting the focus. Interestingly, both of these homes, for clearly that is what they were used as, were facing east just like Emma's was. He watched from about one hundred yards away as a man exited the northernmost structure.

He appeared to be about sixty to sixty-five years old. A grizzled full beard covered his face and chin. The rest of him was sealed up in multiple layers against the cold. A large tree stump at the northeast corner of the house was his destination.

Grizzly picked up the axe which had been thrust into it. Stooping, he grabbed a log, set it upright and took a swat with the axe. He stooped again and inserted a wedge in the log. With one tremendous thrust, Grizzly had four pieces of firewood.

"So that's how you do it," quietly muttered Ian.

Grizzly wasn't done. He picked up one of the four fallen pieces. Holding the quarter in his left hand and choking up on the axe with his right, he proceeded to make kindling with quick, rapid fire strokes. If chopping wood could be classified as an art form, Grizzly was an artist. His relationship with his axe was Babe Ruth with a bat. It was DaVinci with a brush. It was Anna Pavlova in point shoes. The beauty of the work surprised Ian.

Perhaps the clandestine nature of his view was getting to him. He trained his sights on the structure south of Grizzly's. There was a good two hundred yards between the two, but Ian didn't dare draw any closer to either. Surely, these mountain people were wary of movement in their surroundings.

Adjusting his lenses to accommodate the distance, Ian drew in a breath as Emma came into focus. She was kneeling next to an old woman over a nondescript pile of dirt. He couldn't imagine what they were doing. Whatever it was, it was taking all of their energy. He could see their arms and elbows moving about as if they were digging. Digging in this weather in this ground would be no easy task.

A survey of the land surrounding the two homes revealed nothing. No more homes. No more people. Not even Emma's dogs.

Stealing another quick look at Grizzly, Ian determined that he had just enough time left to get home before it grew dark on this side of the peak. He took another bearing with his compass and his cell phone and wrote down the new coordinates. After wolfing down a couple energy bars and consuming the greater part of his water, Ian set off going the way he'd come.

Trying to follow the compass points home in a straight line was not on the agenda. With the amount of snow on the ground, Ian had no idea what hazards lay between his new location and home. Judging by the distance he had traveled north and then west, it would be a much shorter trek home taking the hypotenuse of that triangle. Nonetheless, he would have to wait until spring to try that math.

Ian lay submerged in his bath. His body hadn't ached like this since college. He hadn't laid himself out in a tub since then either. Slowly, he emerged from the warmth of the bath and grabbed his robe.

Emma took that same route every day. Did she lay exhausted in a tub every night, too? Why did she bother coming over to his place every day, anyway? That leg of the journey was entirely self-inflicted. As to Granny and Grizzly, who knew who they were. Or why they were there. Or how Emma was involved with them. Instead of solving puzzles, Ian seemed to be accumulating them.

Dressing and descending the stairs, Ian noticed something he hadn't before: the ticking of the clock. He looked around the downstairs from his vantage point on the stairs. Nothing tickled his fancy. Just thinking about the puzzle, the Sayers book, the meal he'd eat by himself, all seemed to make the tick grow louder.

He grabbed his keys, wrestled on his bomber jacket and navigated to civilization.

Kat handed Ian a hot chocolate, and snuggled up close to him on the couch.

"Ian, let's invite Alfred and his wife. Maybe some of your college friends or folks from my art class. At the very least, we need to have Dad and Kyle here."

Ian took his stockinged feet off the ottoman and set aside the laptop. "Look, Kat, I spend my days and weeks with people I don't know and or don't like. Let's keep Thanksgiving simple and meaningful with just the two of us."

"Wouldn't it be more meaningful to break bread with others and give thanks with others? To share our food, home, time, with others? Isn't that kind of the point of the holiday?" challenged Kat.

"The doorman means nothing to me, Kat. I'm out of touch with my college friends, and your friends, for that matter. You saw your Dad and Kyle when you were in Virginia taking care of your Mother this summer. No, I say it's just you and me and some of my signature smoked turkey." Ian had a way of turning a recommendation, a suggestion, an opinion into

a directive. Was it the result of being an only child, his personality type, or his legal training, or all of he above, Kat wondered.

Kat's voice was shallower, calmer, restrained. "It was five months ago that I saw Dad and Kyle. And we spent most of that time crying and commiserating. My last memories of them are at the funeral with the rain falling on us at the graveside." Kat paused fighting back tears and memories. "We could use this, Ian. Our first holiday without Mom, we need to be together."

Ian finished his hot chocolate and set the mug on the table next to him.

"There's always Christmas, Kat. Only another month away. Let's revisit it then. I'll have less on the docket and can give this my full attention."

Wrapping her hands around her mug, Kat gleaned all the warmth from it she could. She stared down into the cup. The marshmallows had almost shrunk, losing their identity in the swirling mud of chocolate.

"You're making a mistake, Ian. People are the most important thing in the world. Instead of investing in them, you find ways to avoid them. The only compound interest you'll experience is loneliness compounded by emptiness." She got up and left the room.

BETSY BOYD LESLIE

Chapter 10

SADIE'S

There were no empty parking spots within half a block of Sadie's. He parked in front of a fire hydrant fifty feet from the front door, reasoning that there would likely be no buildings consumed in flames tonight. Wedging himself inside the foyer, Ian took a seat with the flotsam and jetsam of Mount Laurel. As far as he could tell, he was the only one dining alone. Damn Kat. Damn her invisibility.

His name was called. He was seated at the best table in the house. It was a cozy bench seat at a window facing the street. Across the street was a picturesque church with wreathed double doors. No wonder he was so melancholy; he had forgotten that Christmas was close at hand. He'd been so engrossed in the Emma dilemma, Kat's invisibility, and now the squatters, that he hadn't given any thought to the day of the week, let alone the day of the month.

"Mr. Campbell?" He'd swear someone was calling his name.

"Mr. Campbell?" Curly peered at him from the end of the table wearing a quizzical expression.

"Dr. Preston, fancy meeting you here," Ian said agreeably.

"I'm sorry if I disturbed you."

67

"No, no disturbing going on. I was just lost in thought. Had you been standing there long?"

"If you call four 'Mr. Campbell's' long, yes. Otherwise, it was a minuscule portion of my day, not to even be considered." Ian had a thought.

"Are you on your way out or on your way in?" he asked.

"In. I was being ushered to a cozy stool on the end of the counter when I saw you sitting here. I thought I'd inquire about your stitching. Is your thumb healing well?" She was smiling as she spoke. Not an ingratiating smile. Not a flirtatious smile. Ian was very familiar with both. It was a simple, honest, sincere smile. Kind of like the brand of cheer he felt in this place.

Ian avoided her question by asking one of his own, "Are you here with someone?"

"As a matter of fact, I was supposed to meet Patty here, the clinic nurse if you recall, but something came up and she had to go straight home. As a result, I am now here *sans* nurse. So, now tell me if your thumb has grown gangrenous or simply fallen off since we sewed it back on."

"Please," Ian gestured to the bench opposite him, "join me and I'll tell you all about my subsequent misfortunes. My nurse didn't show up tonight either, so there's plenty of room. Besides, a bench seat is much harder to fall off than one of those pesky, drafty stools." He found himself smiling back at her. Not an ingratiating smile; he'd given plenty of those. Not a flirtatious smile; he'd delivered those, too. This was a genuine, sincere smile.

"Are you sure? I don't want to intrude. After all, you were totally consumed and entertained before I got here." She asked with her words and her face.

"Absolutely. I've discovered that if I'm alone too much my clock ticks. Besides, it will give me an opportunity to apologize for my behavior at the clinic and regale you with other misadventures."

She slid into the booth.

"You see, I'm a veritable Frankenstein. In addition to my

UPLANDS

thumb being reattached, other limbs and appendages have
fallen off over the years and close friends have found
replacement parts. You see that I'm wearing a lot of clothes. It
has nothing to do with the weather, it's all for concealment. I
wouldn't want to scare the locals." He smiled, enjoying his own
story. Dr. Preston was laughing with him. She leaned back
waiting for more.

"My thumb is fine. All that's left really is a bad memory and
scars of humiliation. And I *am* sorry for my rudeness. Why
didn't you tell me you were the doctor?"

"Did it matter? Would you have treated me differently?"

"Yeah, I would have treated you like the doctor."

"Really?" She leaned in expectantly, "so you have one
bedside manner for nurses and another for doctors?"

"Yes, I mean, no, of course not. Not the way you're
implying."

"I'm not implying anything, Mr. Campbell, just revealing,"
she clarified with a small smile.

A waitress set waters in front of each of them. She grabbed
the wrapped utensils out of her apron pocket and placed them
on the paper placemats.

"So what are you nice folks havin' tonight?" She
accompanied the question with a pencil pointed at her order
pad. "The specials are chicken and dumplin's with a house
salad, chicken pot pie with a side of applesauce and Sadie's
pork chops with a side of greens."

"That settles it for me," responded Ian. "I'll have your
chicken and dumplings."

"And for you, Doc?"

"The usual, Sal."

"With the tea?" asked Sal as she scrawled on the pad.

"Yeah, that would be great."

"You got it." She swept up the menus, stuck the pencil
behind her ear and skirted away.

Ian noticed some curls had escaped the doctor's ponytail. It
really wasn't that bad an effect really. Not a beautiful face, but
certainly not hard to look at either. Most engaging was her

smile. Her mouth was filled with white teeth, obviously not straightened professionally, but acceptably imperfect. When she smiled, it seemed to spread to every part of her face and warm you.

"So, Dr. Preston, in order to avoid the P, and ensure that I don't spew dumplings on you when they arrive, may I call you by your first name?"

"Penelope, but my friends call me Penny." Ian choked on the water he was drinking.

"Oh, I'm so sorry. I mean, not for your name, but, oh, it's a nice name, but for presuming ..." Ian was all but wringing his hands. "Well, there, I've gone and put my foot in it again. So, Penelope it is." Any way he looked at it, Ian had some Ps to pronounce as he ate.

"And what may I call you, Mr. Campbell?"

"Ian. Just plain old Ian."

"That will work beautifully with a mouth full of salad. I'm glad your name is so amenable to poor manners."

With that, Sally placed the house salad before Ian and the hot tea in front of the doctor.

"Are you from around here, Penelope?" Even now Ian could feel himself spitting the Ps at her across the table. He shuddered to think what would happen if he was obliged to use her whole name.

"Penny," she insisted as she prepared her tea. "I was born and reared in a small town south of the Quad Cities."

"Which is ...?"

"Galesburg, if you must know."

She took a sip of tea as he settled into his salad.

"When I decided to go to college, I chose the warmest state that would have me. Florida won. After soaking up all that sunshine for four years, I vowed I'd never go north of the Mason Dixon line again. Famous last words. I ended up getting an offer I couldn't refuse from a school in the Northeast and repeated the whole process." She stopped to chew and acted as though her story was complete.

"And?"

"And, I ended up here."

"Just like that?"

"Well, not entirely *just like that*. I decided to use my new skills where they were the most needed before I had family responsibilities. I ended up in sunny Africa. This was somewhere in between the AIDS crisis and the Ebola crisis, but they still needed a hand." Doc took another bite and looked at Ian for his input.

"So, how did you get to the not-so-sunny destination of Mount Laurel via Africa?"

Doc wiped her mouth, readying her words. "Well, I spent three years there relearning how to live. I may have learned how to prescribe medicine and perform CPR, but I had completely forgotten how important people are to one another. I think Africa was more of a blessing to me, than I was to her. She taught me again the importance of others." She spoke with a settled calm. She looked him dead in the eye, occasionally glancing down at the droplets of water she was rearranging on her water glass.

Ian realized that she wore no jewelry. No rings, no bracelets, no necklace, just a simple pair of sterling silver dangles. He wondered if this was Africa's influence, starving medical student holdovers, or just her.

"Anyway, I had to start making real money again to pay off my loans in earnest. I couldn't go back to life in a big city. Not after living there. So, I looked for a job that wasn't too far north with a needy demographic. With the average temperature what it is and the Appalachian community that utilizes that clinic, Mount Laurel was the best fit. So here I am. It's been my home for the last few years, and I'm glad they'll have me." He nodded mid-chew.

"How about you?"

Ian set down his fork, wiped his mouth with his napkin and leaned back.

"I haven't got nearly the global angle your story does. I mean, shoot, you've got doc smarts, international travel, country girl, city girl, medical school, hippy WHO, bleeding heart .... Your life story's got the makings of a real blockbuster at best, tear jerking Ann Landers at the least. Nope. After that, my life will sound like a real snoozer."

"How about I get you started." She took a sip and began.

"You grew up in the south, but you went to undergrad in Virginia. You graduated at the top of your class, and maybe a little early. Graduate school in New England was the next stop, which you also breezed through quickly. You ended up staying in the north somewhere for work, probably law related. You and your wife decided on Mount Laurel because it wasn't too cold, but you still had the seasons and views." She cocked her head to one side and asked, "Am I even warm?"

Ian squinted at her in bewilderment. "What was that, Sherlock? Are you some kind of clairvoyant or something? Sal feeding you information? Patty do a background check on me or something? And ... AND" he slowed down and added emphasis, "if I am married, why are you sitting here with me?"

Sal thrust a chicken and dumplin's in front of him. "I put the usual on your salad, Doc. And here's some extra dressing on the side. More hot water?"

"Perfect timing, Sal. Thank you, yes." Doc pulled the salad to herself and began rearranging the ingredients.

"Well?"

"If you're really a lawyer, you figure it out," she challenged him. "I don't have any information other than what you gave me."

"Look, I have three enormous, unknowns in my life right now. I've only been reading books lately to which I know the endings, because there is so much mystery in every waking moment. So why don't you just enlighten me, while I sit here with a blank look on my face."

She placed her napkin in her lap, leaned against the cushion behind her and exhaled. "Most people don't chop their fingers off if they're experienced at chopping wood; hence you grew up in the south. Most people aren't going to save a bloodied, ancient UVA shirt unless they spent part of their life and/or life savings there. Since you *do* know how to dress for the cold,

72

but *not* chop wood, that supports my theory that you were some kind of rich kid who didn't need to chop his own wood, but lived in the cold; hence, school. Maybe even boarding school, which would be a stretch since that's some kind of academic relic. Whatever it was, you went through a lot of it quickly, because the birthdate on your charts was not that long ago for a man buying and building on mountains. You're wearing a ring from a New England school, which obviously wasn't your undergrad school, since that was UVA. If you'd gone to UVA for grad school you would've gotten a t-shirt that said as much. That's what the ring and shirt are for; accurately advertising yourself. I'm not sitting close enough to read the fine print, but I would hazard a guess that it's for a law degree. My conjecture is based on three things: First, you wanted to sue me the first time you met me. Second, you ask lots of questions. Third, UVA is an undergrad breeding ground for lawyers. And I'm eating with a married man because ..."

"Because I get off at 7:00 on Fridays and eat supper with her." Sal completed Curly's monologue, set down a basket of burger and fries, pulled off her apron, and took a seat next to the doctor. They both adjusted themselves and exchanged salts and peppers.

"That look is a little less blank than you promised, Ian," the doctor pointed out between sips of tea. Ian looked back and forth between Sal and Penelope. They were both entirely at ease with the turn of events. Ian was still trying to piece it together.

He offered Penelope a narrow look, "I thought you said *Patty* was going to meet you tonight."

"She was."

"You didn't tell me about Sal." He shot a look at Sal, "No offense," he added.

"None taken. Would you pass me the ketchup?"

Ian positioned the ketchup bottle in front of Sal. He sighed in resignation and picked up his fork.

"Sal, would you mind saying grace for us?" asked Penelope.

"Certainly," and before Ian could object, Sal began.

73

"Father, for this food and the many ways in which you have blessed us today, thank You. We know all good things come from Your hand. In Your Son's name we pray, Amen."

The clatter of forks was the only conversation for the next few moments. Ian was absorbed in thought.

"So, how far off the mark was I, Ian?" Penelope engaged him again.

"Well, Penny, if you ever get tired of medicine, I think there's a spot for you with the CIA."

Sal began choking on her food. She came to her own aid in time and began swigging down water while Penelope banged on her back. Ian thought that it sounded as if Sal was laughing as the coughing fits ebbed.

"Oh, and by the way, my name's not Penelope, it's Laura. Laura Tate."

It was Ian's turn to choke.

Chapter 11

GROUNDHOG DAY

Ian awoke to the clatter of dishes. It *was* Groundhog Day. Only this Groundhog Day did not include a Punxsatawney Phil, but an Emma. And she was casting a shadow all over Ian's day. A really long shadow.

He groped around the bed for his robe. In his post-REM state, he tried to remember how he'd spent the last Groundhog Day. A small smile crept on to his face. That's right. He and Sal and Dr. Penelope Preston, aka Laura Tate, had closed down Sadie's. He couldn't remember the last time he'd laughed so hard. Laura had completely caught him unawares. Not just at the clinic, but at Sadie's too. After she and Sal had gotten their laughs in, he had pressed her to explain. It wasn't every day of the week that he called someone by the wrong name, and was encouraged to do so.

"There were two doctors at the clinic the night you came in," she'd explained. "Dr. Preston and I had both been seeing patients. He was supposed to get the next patient to come in, because I'd gotten the last one. So, when Patty checked with you, she meant it when she said that Dr. Preston was going to see you soon. It just turned out that he had a really challenging case come up, so I volunteered to take you. My scrubs don't have names sewn into them, so you had no way of knowing I wasn't the Dr. Preston she'd mentioned. You weren't in the best of moods when I first saw you. You were going on about waiting rooms, lawsuits, and general disgruntlement, so I figured it wouldn't be such a bad thing to continue the charade. After all, if you really did have some kind of mind to sue me, I figured it would go a long way in court if you couldn't even identify me." A smile spread across her face.

"Tonight it was so funny hearing you call me by the wrong name that I had to milk it for all it was worth. Sal and a lot of the locals just call me 'Doc,' so I figured you wouldn't catch on right away. The *coup de grace* occurred when you wanted to call me by my first name. Your excuse was that you didn't want to have to pronounce a name with Ps in it, so that you didn't spit when you spoke. How could I resist? Penelope was out before I could reason with myself. I can't tell you how hard it was not to laugh every time you said, 'Penny' or 'Penelope.' It was so fun I'm going to have try it more often."

Sal was laughing so hard she had given up trying to eat until the story was over.

"Oh, Doc, that was rich. You mean for two weeks now he's been thinking you're Doctor Preston?" Sal could barely get out the question for lack of oxygen.

"Yeah. He even saw me at the grocery the other day and called to me. Of course, it wasn't until he was right next to me that I finally realized he was talking to me, but calling me Doctor Preston." Doc was really enjoying herself. Now, she too was chuckling through the telling.

Ian piped in, "You know, I wondered why you didn't respond to me. I mean I was virtually yelling at you just a car length away. No one gets THAT lost in thought."

"Is that right Mr. Campbell, Mr. Campbell, Mr. Campbell, Mr. Campbell?" ribbed Doc, referring to the scene that had played out just minutes before.

"Touché."

"So, Ian," Sal stopped her thought and raised her eyebrows at him, "I'm not calling you Mr. Campbell after laughing at you that hard," she informed him. "I have way too much dirt on you now to call you anything with a mister in front of it." It appeared to Ian he didn't have much of a say in the matter, so he didn't say a word.

"So," Sal continued, "do you have any idea what Doc Preston looks like?"

"Clearly, no," responded Ian.

Sal began laughing hysterically again. Talking was an impossibility. Doc filled him in. "First, you must know, he's the best doctor around, present company included. He's got a heart of gold and a fanatic following here in town. The reason Sal is getting an extra hurrah out of this is because, well, Larry, Doctor Preston, is in his late sixties. He's like a father to me. To all of us, really."

Sal stared at her.

"She can't stop there," Sal shared. "The man's a bowling pin. He's got an elf frame and a Santa Claus waistline. They kicked him out of the North Pole, cause his combover was creating too much wind resistance. Ol' Rudolph couldn't fight it anymore." And for the *pièce de résistance*, Sal added with finality, "he brought the snow with him! The man can't sneeze without the dandruff settlin'. You'll never see him out of his lab coat for that very reason. I know it."

Laura jabbed her in the ribs. "Okay, blabbermouth, that's enough. You can't talk about Doc Preston that way."

Being in on the joke had worked its magic on Ian. He conjured up an image of a bespeckled, bespectacled, short fat man with Curly Doc's locks. The pent up frustration of the last two weeks was loosed. With Ian on board, Sal's laughter gained new momentum. Doc couldn't fight the both of them. She laughed out loud until her sides hurt.

Ian transitioned from the Groundhog Day of yesterday to the current one with a shower. He would meet Emma on his terms today. He could do this. Especially coming off a night like last night. The magic of the evening hadn't worn off just yet.

"Good morning!" chimed Ian. He rounded the last stair, shot past the closing door of the fridge and stopped short. Instantaneously, the magic was gone.

"What is that?" he yelled.

Carefully swaddled in Ian's monogrammed bath towels, lying on the open oven door, was an animal. The towels already had a sticky, oozy quality about them. The oven was on, emitting a dry warmth into the room.

"Emma, what have you done?" Ian plied. He would have reached out to undo the towels, but couldn't tell what lay amid the filthy folds. Emma beamed back at him from the coffee maker.

"Save whiffle-pig. Almos' die. Think be okay if take care." She shuffled around the kitchen trying not to bump the oven door.

This would explain why she didn't have breakfast ready yet. He had taken a long shower to at least avoid the preparation phase, cutting his time with Emma by at least half. Obviously, the time it had taken for her to find his choice towels and wrap the rodent had made up the difference.

"What in the ... ," Ian held his tongue and closed his eyes. He began again with unconcealed contempt, "Emma, what in the hell is a whiffle pig doing in *my* kitchen wrapped in *my* towels?"

Emma straightened after retrieving a pan from the bottom cupboard. "Whiffle," she enunciated, then pursed her lips together and blew. "Whiffle."

If Ian hadn't been so mad, he could have seen the humor in Emma's response. "Okay," he seethed, "what the hell is a *whistle pig* doing in my kitchen wrapped in *my* towels?" He grew madder by the moment.

"Pig hurt. Emma help." She cracked an egg into the pan, which partially oozed out onto the stove top.

"That's it! Emma, out! Get your pig and get out! Get your

Paxes and Rexes and pig and go!" he glowered at her.

Emma's eyes shot open. She stared searchingly into Ian's eyes. "Emma hurt Ian?"

Ian had the uncomfortable feeling this was a first for her. She hadn't left. She hadn't apologized. She hadn't cried. She hadn't known what to do with his outburst and anger. Clearly, Emma had never experienced it before. Ian felt a sharp sense of shame. Neither Emma's nor his own reaction were what he had expected.

He couldn't retreat now, but he couldn't do what he'd done again. Closing his eyes and breathing slowly, he regrouped with a conciliatory approach. "Emma, your pig ... it needs you to take care of it. You didn't hurt me, I'm just ... worried about your pig, your pig that's hurt. I'll do eggs and bacon. You need to take the pig and go home where you can help it. Okay?" Ian hoped she'd buy it. She did.

"Emma make mess, Emma clean."

"No, I'll take care of it today. You take care of your pig, okay? It will be okay for one day." He tried to sound reassuring. He still felt shameful.

As Emma turned to collect her creature, Ian noticed the two dogs sitting at the edge of the kitchen side-by-side, eyes locked on him. He'd never seen them do that before. They'd never heard him do that before, he figured.

Emma carefully pulled on her coat while trying to hold her charge. She finally had to set it down to finish dressing. Ian was helpless to help her. He knew he should be smiling at her, helping her on with her things, smoothing over what he'd done. He couldn't. He didn't know how to back up and start over.

"See you!" chirped Emma on her way out.

Ian turned off the gas jets, threw the remaining carton of eggs in the trash and sat down to an empty table. He held his head in his hands and cried. It was the second time in two weeks. It was the second time in twenty years.

"You did what?" Ian was incredulous, angry.

"I held her."

"Kat, sitting up with cancer patients is one thing. Holding an infectious disease carrier is entirely different!"

Kat collapsed exhausted into a dining chair. She let her purse fall to the floor while she responded to Ian. *"The baby has no one, Ian. NICU was overwhelmed today and one of the nurses knew me from her stint in Oncology, so she asked if I could just come hang out with all the preemies today. The poor thing is a crack baby too, so she cries incessantly. I'm glad I could give the nurses a hand, but I'm also glad to be home."* She removed her shoes and headed for her closet with Ian in her wake.

"Crack?" Ian flourished his hands as he reached a new decibel. *"All the more reason not to be involved. It's not your job, Kat. You're just a volunteer. You read and color with bald kids and sit up with their parents during surgeries. That's already more than anyone should do, and now you're holding orphaned crack babies with AIDS?"* Ian was getting loud. *"That's not part of your volunteer agreement. Those aren't the terms under which you've agreed to help out."*

They'd reached Kat's closet where she began undressing for a shower. *"So, what you're saying is, that as long as a baby is 'normal' I can help? Where does it say that in my contract, Ian?"*

"What I'm saying is, Kat, there's no just compensation here. Nurses' compensations are what they are because they risk their health and lives. It's part of the terms of their employment and understood hazards of the job. A volunteer is there for emotional benefits. You go there to make yourself and the patient feel better. It's a win-win situation, unless, and it's a big 'unless,' unless you expose yourself to unnecessary harm."

Kat stood before him with a towel wrapped around her bare frame. *"Is that what you think this is? An emotional pat on the back for myself? Is that how you think I leave the hospital every day — feeling good about myself for what I've done that day?"* She narrowed her eyes as she peered at him.

"Subconsciously, yes. That's part of it."

"Maybe I should type this up in a brief and fax it to your office, Ian, because you need to hear me right. I give myself fully and unconditionally for one reason — love. Without sacrificial love put into action, Ian, life isn't worth living."

"And that's what my life will be if I contract something from you — a life not worth living."

"No, Ian, you're wrong. It's not our physical condition that makes life hopeless. We're all stuck with some kind of expiration date. It's our spiritual, emotional condition. We're all dying on the outside, but not everyone is living on the inside." She turned on the shower, closed the glass doors behind her and left Ian standing alone in the bathroom.

BETSY BOYD LESLIE

Chapter 12

DOOR TO DOOR

Staccato raps on the door drew Ian downstairs. He flung the door open to reveal a van parked in front of the house. Emblazoned on the side in wrap were the words, "Door to Door" with pictures of doors splashed around the letters. A man with large biceps and enormous shoulders stuck out his hand.

"Emory at your service, sir. I understand you'd like to get some locks changed?"

Ian eagerly grabbed the proffered hand.

"That's right. I've been having a problem with the current locks. I'll need the front door lock changed," he pointed to the culprit, "and the mudroom door lock." He began making his way past Emory around the porch to the mudroom door. He wasn't sure what Emory might bring in on the bottom of his shoes. If this guy was to end up working on his house, Ian needed to set the precedent right now: All movement between doors and while working on doors, would take place outside.

"Those are some brand spanking new, first-class locks you've got on there now, sir. What kind of trouble you been having with 'em?" Emory's doubting tone put Ian on the defensive.

"They aren't working," Ian snapped with finality.

When they arrived at the mudroom entrance, Emory took the initiative and began working the mechanism to find the problem.

"They don't act up all the time," grunted Ian, "just in the mornings. I just want new locks, okay." Cutting to the chase was required, Ian felt.

Undeterred, Emory took off his "Door to Door" baseball cap and used it to point toward his truck, "Well sir, I'll show you the locks I've got in the truck and you can either choose one of those, or I'll order what you'd like from my supply house."

This wasn't turning out the way Ian had planned. He wanted to *carpe diem* Emma right out of his life. Whatever happened had to happen by 6:30 tomorrow morning.

Ian marched over to the truck. "Let's see what you've got."

Emory opened the back of the truck, appearing to place his hand through a window of one of the wrap doors. Locks of every shape, size and color met Ian's gaze. None of them, however, were of the quality required by Uplands. After thirty minutes of rummaging, Ian gave up.

"What I want simply isn't here. What's the soonest you can have it if I order something?" As much as Ian wanted rid of Emma, Uplands wasn't to suffer for it.

"Our main store is in Hickory, so we can usually get what you want the next day. I'll give you our website address and you can order online." Emory went around to the front of the truck and grabbed a pamphlet and a pen out of the passenger seat. He circled something on the front and handed it to Ian.

"Visit the site I circled. When you get to the 'checkout' phase, be sure to scroll to the bottom before you click 'payment method.' You'll notice there's an installation questionnaire. Be sure to put my name down, 'Emory,'" he pointed to the embroidered name on his shirt in case Ian needed assistance, "and this branch, Mount Laurel. That way it goes directly to me and I can quickly get your order on my truck and over here for installation. It speeds up the process if you put in the branch name and my name. Got that, or do you want me to write it down for you?" He was trying to be helpful.

"I got it. So you'll be back tomorrow? With the locks I order online?"

"That's usually the case, Mr. Campbell. But sometimes parts are out of stock. You'll be able to tell when you place the order if they're in stock or not. I can't remember any occasion where the Hickory store didn't have what the customer wanted, but there's a first time for everything." Emory put his hands in his pockets and leaned back.

"All right. Thanks for coming out and I'll see you tomorrow." Ian turned to go back inside, but had a thought and stopped. If these people couldn't do their jobs right, he'd do it for them. "You've got all the tools you need? You won't need anything special for this installation? No other setbacks when you come out? They'll be installed the same day?" He suspected he looked as strained as he sounded.

"Yes sir, I've got everything I need right here." Emory smiled as he jumped into the driver's seat. "Have a good day, Mr. Campbell and I'll be seeing you real soon."

Ian raced into the house without waving the man off.

Scrolling through private detectives sites was not Ian's idea of an afternoon of adventure. Leisurely retirement this was not. Pushing himself away from the desk, he briefly turned to feel the warmth of the afternoon sun on his cheek as it streamed in the huge glass window behind him. He made his way downstairs for a glass of water and his cell phone. His cell phone rang as he reached for it, catching him off guard. After inspecting the number, he decided not to answer it. When the phone beeped to indicate a message was waiting, Ian reconsidered and listened.

"Mr. Campbell," spoke the phone, "this is Russell Rogers. I did a little investigating for you, just to prove to you I'm not the bad guy. Give me a buzz …"

Ian pressed a few buttons and waited.

"Rogers?"

"Mr. Campbell, glad I caught you," Russell went on. "I've got interesting news for you regarding your Emma."

"She's not MY Emma, Rogers. What did you find out?"

"The building is on your property, but you have not been paying her bills. Her connections are not on the same account as yours. So, any water, gas, or electricity she's been using are on a separate account. Even more interesting, Mr. Campbell, a third party has been paying her bills. "

Ian was cogitating.

"Thanks, Rogers, for looking into this for me. You certainly didn't have to. I checked into it, and you were right; the law is on your side."

"Mr. Campbell, there's a whole lot more to life than the letter of the law. Believe it or not, I try to live my life and conduct business beyond that standard."

"You said a third party was paying her bills. Did you get a name? "

"MacLean. Hamish MacLean. That's all the county records had available, since he pays by cash."

"Did you happen to see anything else regarding my property?" Ian was reflecting on the small village sprouting up in his back forty.

"That's all you mentioned, so that's all I checked on. Thought I'd do a little good faith research."

"Thanks again, Rogers, I appreciate the gesture." With a few conciliatory remarks, they hung up on better terms than the office incident.

Ian stood lost in thought again. He grabbed his water and regained the stairs. Punching in a few letters got him linked to the County Clerk's Office. After finding the number, he dialed them up on his cell phone.

"Hello, have I reached the correct office for Mount Laurel residents?" Ian chirped into the phone.

"Good! Do you have a Phyllis there? No? Well, then who

has been in your office the longest? Maybe I just remembered the wrong name. Could it be Willis?" He'd gotten so good at this tactic over the years, it came as second nature. Pretending to think, Ian kept a hum in his voice as he waited for the clerk to interrupt him. He looked at his watch and noted the time was 10:30.

"Janice? Thirty years? Sure, that was the name! Thanks for reminding me. Could I speak to Janice, please?"

Ian waited for the transfer. He felt as though for the first time in the last month he was getting somewhere with something.

"Hey, Janice, this is Ian Campbell. I purchased a lot back in October of two thousand twelve. Recently, some structures on my land have come to my attention and I just wanted to know if anything was filed by Mr. Waltham, the previous owner, or anyone else regarding those structures."

Janice asked him some questions. While listening, he pulled out a desk drawer and withdrew some documents.

"I think I've got those numbers. I'm used to working with plats, so tell me what numbers you want and I'll try to read them off of my documents."

"Okay, I think I know what you're referring to." He unfolded a large survey of his land and spread it out on his desk. Leaning in to see the numbers, Ian fed Janice information. "In the upper left hand corner I see 'WAL-CAM-22469laurel2012.' Is that what you need?"

Receiving acknowledgement, Ian sat down and leaned back in his chair. Janice was accessing records. He took a swig of his water and imagined what plethora of news Janice would return to him. He was already picturing a name and a face to which he'd be talking tomorrow about Emma's removal. He was imagining the conversation in which he'd break it to the next of kin, or interested party, that Emma Waltham was trespassing and would need to take up residence elsewhere. He was picturing a moving truck driving down the mountain with Emma and her dogs taking up too much room in the front seat for the driver to steer.

"Nothing?" Ian came alive.

"Your records show no other purchases?"

"No other habitations?"

"No other land claims?"

"No other occupants?"

"No liens?"

"Does it show anyone paying for anything having to do with my property?"

"Any encumbrances?" He waited after each question for a specific no. He would rule everything out in case antique Janice had missed something.

"Yes, I know those would have shown up in a title search, but they didn't."

"Janice, have you lived here long?" Ian feigned ignorance.

"Thirty years, wow, that counts. What do you know about Waltham's Peak? Any folk lore or town gossip?" He snatched up his pen and prepared to write Janice's information.

"Emma Waltham, you say?" Ian shook his head and raked his hand through his hair. "Old Man Waltham's girl?"

"So she lives up here somewhere. Do you know where?"

"Do you know who supports her now that her father's deceased?"

"No, I don't mean the town per se, I mean who pays her bills?"

"MacLean? Who's he?"

"Oh, you got that from the town records." Ian rolled his eyes. He felt like this was a Sorry game and he kept getting sent back to Home.

"No idea whatsoever whom MacLean is? Do you know anything else about Emma?"

"Sweet?" Ian found himself repeating Janice for clarification like he would a key witness in a jury trial. He tapped the pointy end of his pencil against the pad of paper he had readied. "No, I don't mean her personality, I mean her whereabouts, where she lives."

"She lives on Waltham Peak," he poised his pencil again. "Yes, we've established that. I mean do you have any other details about her home?"

"No?" The pencil was tapped harder and faster.

"What about support?"

"The town supports her, I know, Janice, thank you. I don't mean moral support or hand-outs, I mean does she have a job or a source of income?" He scratched something into the pad with vigor.

"Slow, autistic, yes, I know, but does she have a job, any way to make money?"

"No?"

Highly doubting it, but asking just the same, Ian ventured, "Do you know anything helpful or useful about Emma or this land?" He held the pencil up by his ear as he listened.

"No? Thank you for your help today, Janice. You've been most, um, agreeable." He creased his brows, hung up and threw the pencil into the hall.

BETSY BOYD LESLIE

Chapter 13

SOCIAL WORKER

"Rosa, you're coming at your usual time, today, right?"

"Good. Could you add to the weekly grocery list fresh salmon, coffee and coffee filters? I want the Gevalia brand Columbian and get the brown filters, not the bleached ones." He waited for her to notate his preferences.

"Yeah, I seem to be going through more coffee than I had anticipated. By the time you get here, I will have had another key made, so I won't have to meet you here now. It will NOT be under the mat. I'll leave it on the mudroom windowpane behind the flower box." About to wrap up the conversation, Ian added, "Oh, and Rosa, if I have any additional instructions for you, they'll be on the kitchen counter next to the coffee maker."

When Rosa arrived she found the key on the windowpane. She also found the list next to the coffee maker, which read:

Rosa,
Fold the bathroom towels using the hotel method: Fold both sides inward, so no edges show.
(A drawing was included for clarification.)
You can place the salmon in the fridge, since I'll be

preparing it tonight.
      Mr. Campbell

   While Rosa was reading up on how Ian preferred for his
bath towels to be folded, and wondering why someone as
OCD as he even bothered to hire a cleaning person, Ian was
on his way to Hickory.

   Ian turned up the heat in the Range Rover as the voice on
the radio warned about falling temperatures. "Three?" Ian
voiced to the empty car. Temps were different in the mountains.
Wind factors, aridity, and elevation all contributed to chilling
one's bones. Crazy, curly doctor Laura had been right; he had
learned how to dress for cold while away at college. That didn't
mean he'd gotten used to it, though. Ian originally hailed from
Florida, which was deeper than "deep South."
   Florida, in Ian's mind, was the perfect state this side of the
Mississippi. In one state, the tourist could find three different
climates: temperate, tropical and sub-tropical. He'd grown up
in the center of the state where little died from freeze, but little
grew in the cold. People said there were four growing seasons
in Florida, if one wanted to garden. He had never been one for
growing things.
   He checked his GPS and estimated the remaining travel
time.
   "An hour to go, Champ. Let's put on some reading
material." Inspecting the CDs in the ceiling compartment, Ian
selected one and gently pushed it into place.
   "It was the best of times, it was the worst of times. It was
the age of foolishness, it was the age of wisdom ..." began his
BBC companion.
   An hour later, Ian rolled into the home office of Door to
Door. The sales associate greeted him from behind the counter
and asked, "What can I do for you today, sir?"
   "I'm Ian Campbell. I called earlier to see if I could come

pick up the locks I ordered."

"Oh, certainly, I'm Rachel. I was the one you spoke to. I set them aside per your request." She reached down into the area beneath the cash register and pulled out a small box. Setting it on the counter, she pushed it over to Ian for his inspection.

"These look like the ones I saw on the website." He picked up the fixtures to make sure they matched. After holding them up to the light and turning them around for a thorough going over, he put them back in the box.

"These won't do. Would you show me another set of the same model?"

Rachel looked perplexed. "What wasn't to your liking, sir?"

"There are some slight mars on the underside of the handle." He began extricating the goods to prove his point. Holding them up for her inspection, he pointed to the errant portion.

Eyebrows creased, she peered at it, moved it, looked Ian in the eye and asked," I'm sorry, but I can't see what you're referring to. Could you point to what you found?"

Quickly, Ian pointed to a spot. Rachel drew the item closer, squinted into the mechanism and shook her head. "Well, sir, I must need a new prescription. I don't see the damage you're referring to. How about I go get another set for you?"

"Thank you, that would be ideal." While Rachel retrieved another set of door locks, Ian rewrapped and replaced the "damaged" ones in their boxes. Just as he finished positioning the boxes on top of each other in perfect symmetry, Rachel walked through the doors with identical boxes.

After another brief inspection, Ian declared, "Looks good, Rachel. What's the damage?" Rachel caught the pun as Ian slipped a credit card from his wallet. After the machine chugged and spit out a receipt, he signed, thanked and left. Rachel drew a breath of relief and shook her head at his departure.

Unlocking the car, he nestled his purchases into the rear compartment of the Rover and relocked the car. He felt a chill as the temperature began its dive to three. While wrestling his collar up against his neck and shoving his hands into his pockets, he checked the traffic and ran across the street to the most local branch of his bank.

Although it was early afternoon, the bank was relatively quiet on the inside. With the wind picking up, people were opting for the drive thru. Going to a bank was beginning to feel like going out to eat. Stanchions and barriers herded the masses, and a sign read, "Wait here to be served."

Disregarding the sign, Ian chose the desk with the woman with the best fashion sense and sat down. The nameplate on the corner claimed the desk as "Ashley Wharton's."

"Hello, Ashley, may I have a check up on my account?"

Irritated at the self-invitation, but trying to be courteous she offered, "Sure, Mr. ...?"

"Campbell. Ian Campbell." He dropped his driver's license on her desk and began reciting his account number.

"What would you like to know?" Ashley asked as she punched in Ian's account number.

"Well, my wife is out of town," too true, Ian thought, "and having the time of her life. I just want to make sure I keep up with her spending. You know how you ladies like to shop." He beamed at her.

"The last five purchases date back to two weeks ago." She aimed the screen at him to show him the data. "The purchases appear to be L.L. Bean, Sadie's Diner, ...

"... Amazon, Harry and David's, and Eddie Bauer," finished Ian. Those were his few Christmas purchases. All his, all to family, all drop-shipped.

"What about prior to those?"

Ashley punched a few keys and the screen revealed new information. Only it wasn't new to Ian. It was all old information – all his purchases.

Kat wasn't joking. She really was invisible.

"Emory, this is Ian Campbell. You came over this morning to install new locks, remember?" Ian sat in the parking lot of Door to Door waiting for the heater to warm the interior.

"Yeah, that's right. Well, I've got the new locks and will be home this afternoon around four. Will you be available?"

"Can't you reschedule them? This is an emergency."

"I know it's unlikely anything will happen, but someone has been loitering around my place in the mornings. I'd feel better if the defunct locks were replaced."

"So the soonest you can install them is when?"

"8:00 a.m.? Can you move that up an hour, say 7:00?"

"Okay, okay, 8:00 a.m. it is. Thanks." He pushed his phone off and set it in the console.

"Burger King this guy is not," Ian announced to no one.

Before heading up the mountain, Ian and his "Tale of Two Cities" pulled up to Ol' Simon's. He clicked off the tale and turned off the car. Grabbing his scarf and wrestling up his collar again, Ian opened the door and braced himself for the onslaught of cold wind. This time the weather guy was right. It was getting cold. Bitter cold.

Simon's place was remarkably warm. The wheezing radiator was more reliable than it sounded, emanating a slow, sure heat. Ian carefully ducked and took a seat next to Pete. It occurred to him that he'd never been in when Pete wasn't there. What was it with this guy? Didn't he have places to go and things to do?

"Howdy, gambler," Pete chided. "Need any info, 'cause I was getting' to the place where I could use another free haircut?"

There were only two other men in the shop, but Ian could swear they too were free haircut recipients. Everything in him wanted to ask, "Yeah, you know where my wife got to? You know who those people are living up on my land? You know why Emma lets herself into my house every morning and makes me breakfast? Got a clue who this MacLean guy is who pays bills for people in cash?"

He found himself asking the last one out loud.

"MacLean, MacLean, now that does ring a bell." Pete

crinkled up his eyebrows and looked at the floor. "Nope, it ain't comin' to me. But I know that name from som'ere." He widened the field.

"Nate, Jeb, Dan'l, you know a MacLean?"

The other occupants scratched their heads and generally looked at a loss. It was the first time Ian had ever heard it quiet in Simon's.

"I remember a MacLean," announced Simon busy on a client, "but I don't want none o' you guys cuttin' my hair." He pointed his scissors at them for emphasis.

"Whatcha got, Simon?" Now Pete was hot on the chase, as well. Here was a piece of information that had eluded him.

Simon resumed his clipping. "I recall that Old Man Waltham had a gardener who had a Scottish name and a brogue that went with it. Seems he'd come over for some kind of movie bit that didn't pan out like he'd hoped. He worked for Waltham in the city and got recruited to come out here when they installed all their fancy plants."

Pete had an epiphany. "That's it! I don't recollect what became of him, though. You, Simon?"

"Campbell here's offerin' free haircuts, not cruise line tickets." Redirection was impossible at this point. From there the conversation fell into a discourse on which of Sadie's specials was better, the Chicken 'n' Dumplin's or the Chicken Pot Pie.

Somehow, listening to talk of Sadie's and warm, thick, pasty foods like these, made Ian homesick. For what, he wasn't sure. He just knew he didn't like the idea of going home to a cold salmon and an empty house.

"Hey, darlin'," greeted Sal, "can I get you a seat by the window?"

Sal called everyone "darlin'" Ian noticed, but it warmed him nonetheless.

"Sure, Sal. That sounds great." He unraveled his scarf and pulled off his jacket as he followed her to his seat from last week.

"Thanks, Sal." Ian meant it. He relaxed into the vinyl seat and stared out the window at the same wreaths on the same doors as the week before. Passersby obscured his vision and snapped him out of his reverie. He found himself running through all the points of the dumplings and pot pie debate that were recited at Simon's. When Sal showed up, he'd be ready.

"So what'll you have, Mr. Campbell? Our specials tonight are pork chops with a side of au gratin or pecan crusted trout with edamame beans."

"I'll have the dumplings, Sal," Ian ordered with confidence. He had a quiet, calm feeling he hadn't felt in a long, long time.

"Those are tomorrow's specials, darlin'. This here's Wednesday and our specials are pork chops and trout."

Ian simply stared at her.

"I recommend the trout, Ian," he heard from his left. He turned to see Curly Crazy Doc herself.

"Trout it is, Sal. And we'll keep your seat warm for you."

"You know what I call you when you're not looking?" Ian asked the doctor seated across from him.

"Penelope Preston?" She let out a laugh as she said the name.

"You wish. No, I call you the Crazy Curly Doc."

"I've been called worse."

"Doubt it. You're like the Mother Theresa of this century. Who could possibly want to call you a name?"

"Wealthy, spoiled, city guys for one."

"Well, since there aren't any of those around here, you're safe in Mount Laurel."

Sal dropped off their drinks on her way to another table.

"So, where's nurse Patty tonight?"

"She usually only eats with me on Thursday nights. It's just Sal and me on Wednesdays."

"You eat here every night?"

"Usually. I don't on the weekends, but generally on

weekdays. I work long shifts, so by the time I get off work, I'm exhausted. I don't have the energy to make my own meals and I don't feel like going home to an empty house to eat them. So, I typically eat here and go home for bed and bath." She was leaning back into the seat, perfectly comfortable. He wondered how many times she'd sat in that very seat for her evening meal. He wondered where Kat was eating her evening meals.

"Besides, I usually eat salads. By the time I buy all the stuff I want in them, I can't eat it up fast enough to merit the grocery bill. So, I might as well pay someone else to do that grocery shopping and salad building for me. Besides, Sadie's kind enough to make salads especially for me. It's a win for Sadie and a win for me."

"Sounds like a perfectly symbiotic relationship. There's the shark and remora, the African Oxpecker and, well, the ox, and Sadie and Crazy Curly Doc."

"That's it!"

Sal slid three meals across the table, sat down and began reciting the ownership.

"That's a Tate Salad for you," as she slid Doc's salad over to her.

"A Pecan Trout for you," and she handed Ian his napkin-wrapped utensils.

"And a Dumplin's for you, Sal girl," she recited as she pulled the plate to herself.

Ian shot her a look. "Dumplin's? But I thought ..."

The women broke down laughing.

The next morning was going to be blisteringly cold. The low, as Ian made his way up his mountain, was now officially three degrees. Throughout the evening, the wind was to whip through Mount Laurel dropping several inches of snow and several degrees in temperature. Thankfully, Ian reflected, he had purchased the best thermal windows money could buy and added insulation beyond code. Howl it may, but he wouldn't feel a thing.

He was frustrated that the locks hadn't been replaced. That would mean at least one more morning of Emma's bacon and eggs. His only consolation was the light at the end of the tunnel - locking her out.

To decrease the shock, he set his alarm to go off before Emma arrived. He would make breakfast himself, thereby thwarting her need to feed.

Kat looked absolutely stunning as she stood against the amber lights of the tree in her black evening gown. If his memory served, it was number nine, which he'd paired with the Lucida platinum diamond dangles. Tonight was the annual Christmas Gala event, sponsored by their firm every year. They invited all the noteworthy clients who had helped fill their court calendars and coffers. Ian's clients, the ones who were the hardest to track down, were the real bread-and-butter of the firm, which created a conundrum for Ian, since he hated attending these events. Their money may have come from offshore accounts under pseudonyms, but it spent the same. Or, in Ian's case, it saved the same.

Kat worked the room. Not as a networker, but as a social worker. She was genuinely interested in each person there. To an extent. If she sensed narcissism, or unkindness she moved on, but she gave everyone the benefit of the doubt. Ian spied her shaking hands with Stephen Woodrow, his current client up for embezzlement and a host of other financial crimes, and wondered how long it would be before she sized up his selfishness and moved on. Perhaps he'd give her a hand.

"Evening, Mr. Woodrow. Enjoying the spread? After all, this is all about you." Ian flashed his lawyer smile. "Kat, you ready to go?" He placed his hand on her hip as he inquired.

"You have a charming wife, Mr. Campbell. I've been enjoying our discussion on philanthropy. It seems your wife has an interest in assisting the physically downtrodden. I applaud that," said Woodrow.

"Yes, Kat has a heart of gold. It can be quite costly." Ian's candor provided the intended meaning to his comment. Mr. Woodrow took Ian in quickly before continuing.

"*My daughter was recently cared for by your wife, Mr. Campbell.*" Ian was stunned. "*I would even venture to say that your wife saved her life.*"

"*How's that,*" asked Ian, "*she's just a volunteer?*"

"*Emily had just undergone a treatment and had been returned to her room. In the short time it took for my wife to come home and me to relieve her at the bedside, Emily had a seizure. Your wife was the only one in the room when it happened, and knew to turn her on her side and hold her down. When I arrived, there were three nurses and a doctor responding to a code on the monitors. Were it not for your wife's quick thinking, my Emily would not be here today.*" As he spoke, his eyes moved from Ian to Kat. As they rested on her, he took her hand and kissed it. "*Thank you, Mrs. Campbell.*"

Ian and Kat drove home in silence.

Eight hours later found Ian at the stove preparing an omelet. Sputtering was heard from the coffee maker as it spewed the last of the brown liquid into the carafe.

Snow, and lots of it, was all Ian saw as he continuously glanced out his kitchen window to the north in anticipation of Emma's arrival. She was late. He put the last of the cut vegetables on the waiting eggs. Coffee fell into his cup of waiting cream and sugar. Emma still hadn't appeared. The omelet was plated and garnished, and still there was no sign of the trio. Ian ate his omelet in his silence.

Chapter 14

WINTER OF THE CENTURY

The roads were closed. Mount Laurel was buried in a foot of snow. The National Weather Advisory had warned of epic snowfall and record-breaking temperatures, not only for this week, but the entire winter. It was to be the winter of the century.

Emory of Door to Door called to say he wouldn't be up the mountain today. He added that considering what the weatherman was saying, it might be a little longer than that. He pointed out that if the roads were closed, there wouldn't be any way the bad guys could get to him anyway. Little did he know, thought Ian.

He parked himself in front of the fire, trying to rely on ambient heat, rather than central. By the looks of it, this was going to be a white winter, after all.

He spent the day contacting detective agencies, washing laundry and cleaning up after the housekeeper. All day the snow fell. All day he trudged into it to retrieve more wood for his fire. The wood shed was just beyond his porte cochere, requiring a good thirty minutes to don the requisite clothing, trek through the accumulated precipitation, find the wood pile, collect quarters and pile enough up for the next several hours on his porch. No wonder wood was the tie-breaker in the survival shows, he considered as he made the latest slog through the slush and deposited his load. The woodpile was becoming alarmingly low. If the flurries kept up and the temperatures kept falling, he'd have to do some more chopping. He didn't relish the idea. Not after the stitches fiasco. Especially not in this weather.

Brushing himself off inside the mudroom and depositing his gear, Ian centered his boots on the mat for the fourth time that day. He filled the electric kettle and prepared himself some hot tea. It was too late for coffee, but too early for anything harder.

While the pot was on, he retrieved the quarters he'd left by the back door to drip dry and placed them in the fireplace. Doing so required a re-assemblage of the existing fire using his favorite tool. He glanced at Kat's photo by the door. She had given him this tool last fall.

They'd come down for a long weekend to try out the fireplace for the first time. Although the house had been done for a few months, it had been completed in late spring, too late for an inaugural run of the chimney and hearth. So Ian had Shelly reschedule all of a Friday's appointments, and they came down with a bottle of Ian's favorite vintage.

When they'd settled in with Ian's jazz in the background, his hearth in the foreground, and his favorite vintage cradled in his hands, Kat came and settled down next to him. She handed him a wrapped gift. It was in a long, narrow, rectangular box wrapped in grocery store paper bag and tied with muslin strips. It was typical Kat; interesting yet frugal.

He had unwrapped it with skepticism to find his new favorite tool - the firehawk. He'd never been much of an outdoorsman. He'd never been a boy scout. He'd never even really enjoyed the snow or the cold that accompanied it. "Tolerated" was really the best way to describe Ian's attitude toward any element other than seventies and sunny. But this tool reached a primitive part of him that unleashed new longings. He was surprised at Kat's ability to gift him so well, and excite something untapped in him.

He reached for the firehawk. After manipulating the glowing cinders, he positioned the new quarters and blew the fire into life.

How had Kat eluded him all this time? Clearly, she had been planning and preparing for some time in order to have been so effectively invisible. There was absolutely no trail in regard to finances. Kat hadn't used one credit card, debit card or check from their joint accounts since the day he'd left Boston. Not one financial transaction had taken place in the last two months that hadn't been at his initiative. The financial trail wasn't just cold, it was frigid.

Every dollar, every dime had been accounted for. He knew, because he'd been watching their accumulation, like a bookie watches a finish line. While today's research had lead to dead ends, he was confident that tomorrow's would provide the lead for which he had been looking. He was going to review all the phone records on their respective phones. The records were open and ready for his perusal, but he wasn't. They'd have to wait until tomorrow when he was fresh for the hunt. As soon as he dodged the Emma bullet, he'd get back to work, this time with phone numbers rather than banking numbers. Cursorily, he'd checked them before. However, he hadn't been looking for what he was going to look for this time.

Ian closed the lid to his laptop, stood up from his perch and stretched. His sock feet padded to the hearth, where his tired hands stirred the dying embers into life for the last time that day. He made his way to the mudroom window and looked at the thermostat on the pane.

He startled himself by exclaiming out loud, "Ten?" With a flick of his wrist, the outdoor light came on illuminating a winter wonderland. The snow came up to eighteen inches on the landscape. It was still falling. He topped off his tea, swiped on the weather station at his kitchen radio panel and listened to the robotic voice forecast his future.

"… dropping into the teens for Mount Laurel and setting a new record," he heard it say between sips. "Precipitation between six and twelve inches expected for the next twelve hours in varying parts of the Laurel Chain. Weather advisories are in effect for the Laurel Chain and outlying areas. County schools will be closed Friday the twentieth."

The kids are going to get an early start on Christmas break, thought Ian. With the kitchen clean and lights off, Ian made his way upstairs and showered. Pulling on his pajamas, he reached for his alarm, fingered the knob to make sure it was set and leaned back against the pillows.

It hadn't felt like a productive day. It began in downtown Mount Laurel at the County Land Office. With the help of an ancient assistant, he had looked up the applicable statutes and codes regarding Squatter's Rights. He then located Old Man Waltham's deed and determined that there were no encumbrances or provisions for Emma or anyone else on Waltham's land. In addition to the documents relating to the land, Ian had visited a number of offices and viewed pages and pages of microfiche until he'd located a copy of Waltham's will. Pete had been right about the terms and the trust.

Clearly, Waltham had made provisions for those he loved, but none of them included the land Emma and her friends now lived on. This would make Ian's claim and eviction much easier to carry out. With copies of the will in hand, Ian made his way to the courthouse, filled out a Complaint in Summary Ejection (he liked the sound of that word), wrote and signed a check, watched the clerk date and stamp the form, and danced a little jig out of the office. He was beginning to see a light at the end of the tunnel.

When a faint hint of regret made its presence known, Ian decided on the more magnanimous move, and asked about local elder and incompetent care at the Information Desk. A smiling face handed him a sheet of contacts. The group home names and addresses would come in handy when it was time to issue the directive for Emma to leave. This way, Ian figured, he would have a place to recommend the police take her when they came to get her. After all, he didn't want to just leave her out in the cold. As for the others, whoever they were, they would have to fend for themselves.

Reflecting on the morning's success, Ian noted that finding Kat's cold trail that day had been less fruitful. He'd burned a cord of wood and gleaned no new facts about her whereabouts. Then again, he'd completely ruled out a few things: Kat hadn't used any of his money, or "theirs" rather. She hadn't continued to use any of their accounts, homes, phones or anything they jointly owned. He'd even tried contacting Alfred, who'd had the audacity to retire, and spoke to the building manager instead, only to discover that Kat's car was still in the garage, but he hadn't seen hide nor hair of Kat. Neither the car, nor the penthouse, had been touched since the day he left. It was eerie. Kat was gone as if she'd never been there.

It was eerily quiet when Ian awoke. It was always quiet, but today was deafeningly so. He strode to the windows overlooking the valley. What had once been a gently sloping valley was now a veritable Olympic ski run. He'd never seen so much snow in his life. The treetops poked above the blanket as if gasping for air in the suffocating layers. Surely, there had been more than twelve inches in his "outlying area."

He grabbed some jeans, jammed his feet into his thickest wool socks, threw on a flannel shirt and covered it with his warmest wool sweater. The clock glared 6:48. He wanted to be downstairs ready to intercept Emma when she appeared.

Thirty minutes later, Ian sat alone at his breakfast nook nursing a cup of coffee. He glanced out the back door one more time to reassure himself that Emma was nowhere to be seen. The snow must have kept her away ... again. Nonetheless, he was surprised considering her dogged determination to provide him with bacon and eggs on a daily basis.

He proceeded to ready his repast. The omelet wasn't quite as good as the day before, but enough to see him through until lunch. With the dishwasher emptied and the breakfast dishes in place, Ian finished putting the kitchen in order and set to his detective duties with a will.

The last six months worth of phone bills were retrieved electronically. Each and every text and call was reviewed. If it was an unknown source, Ian cross-referenced the number with his work files. If the number still wasn't identified, he looked them up through the national networking system he had subscribed to and used as a service with his firm. Shelly was typically the one to employ them at work, but Ian had needed to access it so frequently in tracking down clients and witnesses, he was well–versed in its utilization.

By lunch he had determined that every single number that appeared on Kat's phone for the last six months had either been his own or her family members'.

Kat had few friends, at least few that she introduced to Ian. He knew that she occasionally went out with some of her artsy friends after a class, but she had never developed close friendships with any of them. Ian had forbidden it. They weren't the kind of people he thought their like should be associating with. It wasn't good for business, either.

Ian was flummoxed. He decided a jaunt to assess the wood situation and a hearty lunch would get his creative juices flowing. He hated this Kat and mouse game. He'd come up with a new approach, another angle. He had to.

While punching in the numbers on his cell phone, Ian filled his glass with some room temperature Le Croix. Stepping over to his new office in front of the downstairs hearth, Ian settled in and propped up his feet. Absentmindedly, he picked up a pile of papers and began leafing through them as he waited for the other line to ring.

"Hello, Mark, have I reached County Services?"

"Good. Listen, my mountain road hasn't been plowed in two days. To whom would I speak to rectify this situation?"

"That's a new one on me. You mean the county doesn't

maintain its own roads? Well, then, could you get me in touch with the people who do?"

"City or state?"

Ian jotted down some numbers. "Do you know anyone in that office you could refer me to? Cheryl? How about the other office? Skyler? Oh, Tyler, got it. Thank you, Mark. I appreciate the help."

Ian punched in some more numbers and pasted the phone to his ear with his shoulder. He rearranged more papers next to his laptop. As he leafed through the papers, he neatly dropped some on the floor in a discard pile. He came to attention as a voice interrupted his thoughts. His finger pressed the one and replaced the phone next to his ear.

"Hello? Could you please connect me to Cheryl in maintenance?"

"Hi, Cheryl, this is Ian Campbell on Mount Laurel. Mark over at county services told me you'd be able to help me out. Could you find out where I am on your plowing to-do list for today?" His tone was reserved, but optimistic. That changed.

"Well, if Mark at County doesn't have the list, and you in City Services don't have the list, then who does?"

No more pillaging the papers, no more rooting through laptop numbers, Ian was fully engaged with Cheryl.

"And who could I ask for there? Are you *sure* that's where the winter maintenance decisions are made? Great," he said, but not convincingly. "Could I have a contact name for that department?"

"Thanks." Ian pushed a button and redialed.

"Maintenance? Yeah, may I speak to Tyler, please?"

"Hey, Tyler, I've been looking for you all day. It seems you're the man with the magic list. Could you tell me where we are on your plowing list for today? The road is Mount Laurel Pass off of 129. Thanks for checking."

"You mean our road isn't even on your plowing map for today?"

Ian certainly had a way with words. He *was* the citizenry of his mountain. From a half mile from the peak to the top, there was no one but Ian. Ian grimaced and rolled his eyes as he recalled that there were, indeed, other residents of his mountain. Three to be precise. Suddenly, his "we" argument took on new gusto.

"Listen, if you guys don't get up here in the present to near future, we will have been snowed in for three days." His voice was taking on a new tenor. A moment passed while Ian gave him an opportunity to fix his error.

"Tyler, my road needs to end up on that list before I hang up." Ian paused before continuing.

"I'm glad you all have your priorities straight, especially in light of the fact that we have so much more snow on the way. I know you've got 18,000 folks to consider in Mount Laurel. I can appreciate that you have 3 state highways and 2400 miles of pavement in town that needs plowing. Yes, I know we've had 20 inches of snowfall in the last 2 days – I'm looking at it – all 20 inches of it - because it's STILL HERE!" Ian was starting to lose it.

"Look, Tyler," Ian took in a deep breath and released it as he paced the floor. "Would you let me speak to your manager for a moment? Maybe he and I can come to an understanding about ..." Ian pulled the phone away from his ear to look at the screen. The screen showed no bars.

Feverishly pushing buttons, Ian kept checking for Tyler.

"Hello? Tyler? Hello?"

"Damn!" The phone was hurled into the couch. Ian turned to check the status of the snow. He walked over to the kitchen radio and stabbed at buttons until the metallic voice rattled off the statistics.

"Continuous snow flurries for the next twenty-four to thirty-six hours. Blizzard conditions are expected in some parts of North Carolina, Virginia and West Virginia. Temperatures are expected to drop steadily in Watauga, Cherokee and neighboring counties. National weather advisory is currently in effect."

While the voice carried on, Ian found his phone again and wandered around his house looking for service.

"Be advised, communications are tenuous for most of the

tri-state area. Remaining indoors is advised."

"This is unbelievable!" Ian ranted, as he took the stairs two at a time. He tried his desktop and found it dead. He ran to his bedroom and noted the lights blinking on his alarm clock.

"You've got to be kidding!" He shouted to no one in particular.

The lights were out, but he hadn't noticed. It was midday, the sun, albeit hidden, had been reflecting off the snow into the vast windows in front of his makeshift office. As such, he hadn't even bothered with a lamp. Now he was keenly aware of a lack of lighting.

"What is this, Pokeyville? It snows for a while and the place comes to a screeching halt?"

For the remainder of the day, Ian chopped wood and readied himself for a few hours without electricity. He spent hours chopping until the pile was ample. The empty stall of the porte cochère, where Kat's car would have been, was the perfect setting. He had hauled the cords out of the snow and under the roof. It was still remarkably cold, and the snow managed to drift in, but it was a sight easier than wrestling with the wood while standing in two feet of flurries.

Placing his latest cuts on the racks, Ian rested his hands on his hips and surveyed the results. The two semi-circular log racks on either side of his mudroom door sonorously smiled back at him.

He considered how apropos the image was. The two log racks had been one of the most difficult purchases to get in place at Uplands. They had come from the northeast by truck completely assembled. After all, they were solid steel, weighing two hundred pounds each. There weren't many carriers willing to make the haul and delivery with something so cumbersome. The delivery itself had put him at half again the cost of the items. It had been worth it. When he saw the finialed steelwork up against the barren walls of the house under the protection of the porte cochere roof, he had been pleased. He was pleased now.

As he stood gazing at his handiwork, it suddenly struck him

how relaxed he was. He had been deeply agitated, incredibly frustrated and downright angry about his detecting results. And now he was snowed in. The effort it took to turn his cords into quarters and kindling had been therapeutic, albeit his stitching had smarted. The days and nights of Kat and Emma stress that had built up or seeped in had been transferred to the wood he saw stacked before him.

He grabbed the axe and wedge to return it to the storage room on the other side of the porte cochere. He came out wielding a large bin labeled "emergency supplies." Fumbling with the handle to the mudroom, he wrangled the bin through the door and pulled the door shut with his boot. Unpacking the bin on the kitchen counter, Ian removed lanterns, matches, a camping stove and other gear one might need for a cold, dark overnighter. He placed the items in cupboards or strategic places for their purpose.

Meanwhile, the shadows grew longer and the house grew darker. Ian lighted a lantern and sat down with a bottled water. Rehydrated, he added some fuel to his fire and stirred the embers into life. He surveyed the room and considered his next plan of action.

The next task involved taking inventory of his refrigerator. He removed the food, which had the least shelf life, a salmon filet and some greens. The Smeg fired into life and he silently praised himself again. He smiled for the first time that day as he released his catch into the pan. Salt, pepper, a lot of butter and some freshly grated parmesan brought his salmon to seared perfection. Some tossed greens and olive oil completed the fete.

Two lanterns on either side of his workstation allowed him to see the end results of his day's detecting work. None of it had lead him to Kat. Discouragement would have set in, but there was one remaining thread of hope, which would have to wait until tomorrow. That is, if electricity was restored. The battery had finally given out on his laptop. Fitting a headlamp to his forehead, he made his way to the basement doors near the woodpiles. A brief inspection revealed a ready and willing furnace; another precautionary measure that would come in handy when the grid failed, warming his home and feeding his pride.

When Ian awoke at six, he wasn't surprised. With the physical exertion of the day before and the lack of light inside, he'd gone to bed early.

He listened for kitchen clanking, but heard none. He was almost sorry he didn't. Making his way to the windows overlooking his newly dubbed ski slope, Ian couldn't believe his eyes. There was at least four feet of snow on the ground and it was still falling. The blinking clock affirmed that there was still no power. Had he missed that, the frigid temperature of the room would have reminded him.

Fire came first. It was too damn cold to ignore. Gathering wood from outside the mudroom door and grabbing some discarded Wall Street Journal was the matter of a moment. A fire was raging in the hearth in no time, taking the edge off the chill. Thoughtfully perusing the landscape out the mudroom door, he considered the density of the snowfall. There was no way Emma could traverse this. He was beginning to smile at the unexpected coup, but hesitated. He had an unfamiliar feeling. A feeling he couldn't identify.

Thinking back to his surreptitious visit to Emma's, he remembered a stove in her home, but no fireplace. And there certainly wasn't any wood stacked at her place to feed one. How was she managing? Ian tried to recall every aspect of her little home's interior. Surely her father would have planned for a day like this. Wouldn't he? Surely there had been days like this before that included too much snow and too little warmth. Try as he might, he could not recall a way in which Emma could brave these elements in that cottage. His relief at not having to deal with Emma was quickly being replaced by something else: concern.

BETSY BOYD LESLIE

Chapter 15

FEVER

He tried his phone again, for naught. While filling a pot with water, firing up the gas flame on his stove, and setting the pot on to boil, Ian came to a decision. Grabbing his backpack from the mudroom, he hastily threw in some granola and energy bars from his kitchen cabinets. Simultaneously, he prepared a high protein breakfast and packed his backpack. Dishes were stuffed into the sink as he quickly cleared the kitchen. Another trip was made to the storage room adjoining the porte cochere. This time he wielded a pair of snowshoes and poles. He trudged through the snow that had made it into his covered parking and brought his equipment indoors. After going back upstairs and dressing for the tundra, he checked and rechecked the contents of his backpack. A compass, rope, hand warmers, bottled water, food, and numerous other items made their way into his backpack. When the packing was completed, he drew paper and pen out of a kitchen drawer and scribbled a hasty note.

Left at 7:00 a.m. December 22nd on foot. Went NW approximately two miles to Emma Waltham's dwelling.

He wasn't sure who exactly he expected to see it, or for that matter care. Donning hiking boots, hat, scarf, and jacket, he stuffed his mittens into his pockets, and with his pack thrown over his arm, he grabbed his snowshoes and poles and closed the door behind him.

Two hours later, he was knocking on Emma's door. He was sweating under his layers, a survival no-no. But the exertion had gotten the best of him, and he didn't know what to do to counteract the problem. His jacket was now stowed on his pack and his next layer was holding in the moisture he'd generated. In spite of the volume, the going had been easier than he thought it would be. His snowshoes kept him above most of the drift. It was not yet noon as he peered into the sky to check the progression of the sun against his own.

He rapped on the door again. The cabin was as silent as a tomb. He lifted his feet out of the hole they'd been making in the snow, and plodded over to a window. Although it was curtained, he could see between the panels. All lights were off and no other lighting was visible. Nothing stirred. Ian cupped his hands over his eyes and leaned against the window to shut out the glare of the snow. The bed was unmade and meal dishes were on the table, as if she had been interrupted in the middle of a meal before her departure. There was no sign of human or canine life.

He made his way back to the door and tried the knob. It was unlocked.

"Hello?" he called as he leaned in to the dwelling.

A quick survey confirmed that the room was empty. He checked the dishes and the house to look for clues as to where she was or when she left. Admittedly, he didn't know Emma well, but he knew her well enough to know that this was out of character for her. She never left a dish unwashed. She never left a room untidied. Sometimes, she never left.

The meal appeared to be the remains of a breakfast, but it certainly wasn't today's, perhaps not even yesterday's. There were no other clues to go by other than the sheer chill. No one had been here anytime in the last twenty-four hours.

As an afterthought, Ian looked through a drawer for an address book or a list of important numbers. Considering the fact that there was no phone or electronic equipment of any kind, he doubted his search would yield positive results. He was right. There was nothing to indicate that she had a friend, a next of kin, a life.

He checked her pantry for food and found a few morsels he could pack to go. His goal of finding Emma had taken on new dimensions. How he was going to go about doing this was beyond him. But what had been mild curiosity, now turned to slight alarm.

He mentally retraced his steps. Had he passed footprints on the way? Had he passed her? He didn't think so. If he had seen anything other than billowy snow, he would have noticed. *Any* contrast in that landscape would have stood out. Whether it was an indention in the pack or a person on foot, he would have noticed. Had she fallen and been covered by snow? If she'd set out two mornings ago on a bacon-and-eggs mission, enough snow would have fallen in the interim that it would cover a body by now.

He began to panic, when another element came to mind calming him: the dogs. Even if something had happened to Emma rendering her immobile, there wasn't enough snow on the planet to cover her and two living leviathans. No, thankfully, that scenario had to be dismissed.

The next most likely scenario was the mini-village to the west. The one he'd come upon with the hermit and the old lady. Obviously, Emma had a friendly relationship with those people. They all behaved as if she was part of their environment, part of their community. After all, you only dig with people you know.

He set out in that direction, careful to sip as he searched. He did not see any footprints or tracks of any kind. There had been too much recent snowfall for that. He watched for landmark trees to keep his bearings. The ocean of white was disorienting. He stopped at a boulder and took out his compass. It was rubber-banded to the notebook he'd used the last time he had trekked this way. Although the GPS latitudes and longitudes weren't helpful, his other notes were. He carefully followed those, the track of the sun, and his instincts. He tried not to rely too much on the latter. Nature walks weren't his forte.

Give him a hostile witness and he could needle the truth or an obvious lie out of him. Hire him to get out of a million dollar embezzlement charge and he would not disappoint. He could even whip up a mean salmon or filet mignon. Move past a desk, a dial pad, or a door and things were apt to get dicey.

He turned to replace his compass in an outer pocket of his pack when he looked down and saw them. Footprints. They were on the lee side of the boulder and looked to be the size of dinner plates. They were either bloodthirsty, rabid wolves or lethargic, leviathans named Pax and Rex.

Ian felt a sense of relief wash over him. Temporarily. As quickly as he felt success, the feeling of failure invaded. Just because he knew he was on the right track, didn't mean something positive was on the end of this trail.

He slung his pack, rechecked his snowshoes and began again. Within twenty minutes, he saw smoke curling above the pines before him. He followed the smoke. Another fifteen minutes brought him to the door of what he thought was the old lady's house. A fallen tree stood between this cabin and the next. He didn't recall that from his last visit. The identifying vegetable garden, wood stack, and water barrel were erased. The only other landscape to let Ian know he'd been here before was the woodcutter's cabin just north of this one.

Ian knocked on the door. The sound was quickly absorbed by the enveloping white. A few more moments lapsed before a face emerged between the door and its jam. It was Emma. Her haggard visage brought to Ian that now familiar, yet odd mixture of relief and panic.

"Emma, are you okay?" asked Ian.

"Pearl sick," she replied. Another face peered out at Ian. It was Rex coming to check the intruder. Apparently, Ian passed his test, because he quickly disappeared again.

Emma stepped back and beckoned Ian in with her eyes. Before Ian could see his surroundings, he smelled them. He almost retched. The air was close. The room was warm. The fever was palpable.

On a bed in the corner of the room lay a small child. Ian guessed that she was no more than eight. Her eyes were closed, her bright red cheeks set off by the pasty pale surrounding them. Seated next to her in a weathered rocking chair sat the old woman. They both appeared to be asleep.

"Emma," whispered Ian, "who are these people?"

"This Pearl," as she pointed to the child, "and this Ruby," she said as she motioned to the woman in the rocker. "Pearl sick long time. Ruby and Emma tired." Emma completed her statement and stared at the bed as if nothing more needed to be said to estimate the situation.

"Why are you here?" asked Ian as he unbuckled his snowshoes.

"Mr. Mac come get Emma to help Ruby," Emma answered as she licked her lips. The stale room was sucking the moisture off of Ian's lips, too.

"Emma, you mean the guy next door went to get you to help these people - and you came?" Ian was perplexed. "When was this?"

"Monday morning."

They both stood in the center of the room exchanging looks. That was three days ago.

"Is the little girl better?"

"No, Emma take her into town." Emma pointed to something on the floor. Whatever it was, it looked as if it was in a state of construction. "Pearl real sick," Emma continued, "No more medicine now."

She sat down on the floor and resumed her project. Ian stood staring trying to assess the situation. How sick or desperate did someone have to be to hail Emma for assistance?

Emma appeared to be weaving something using vines.

"Emma, you say this girl is sick. What's wrong with her?"

"Fever," replied Emma not taking her eyes off her work.

"How high is her fever?"

"Hot. Pearl real hot."

"What does the thermometer say?"

"No fermometer. Just hot."

"Criminey, you mean you guys don't have a thermometer around here, no modern medical supplies of any kind?"

"Fermometer broke in mouth."

Ian absorbed the idea. "Was it a glass thermometer with a red line running up the inside?"

"Yes."

"Did silver bubbles come out in her mouth when it broke?"

"Yes."

Another dilemma was escalating. Ian had never felt such panic or pressure as he had for the last month. And he was retired.

"Where is the man who lives next door? Did he go get help?"

"Mr. Mac broke leg. Now Emma get help for Mr. Mac, too."

"What? You mean he's over at his house with a broken leg?" Ian was doing all he could to keep his whisper to a faint yell. The last thing he wanted was this squatter to wake up and drill him with questions when he had so many of his own.

"Emma, take me to Mr. Mac's." For the first time he realized that both dogs were surrounding the child's bed. One was at the foot, the other where her feet would land were she able to get out of bed. They looked at him knowingly. Ian wondered if they weren't more aware of the child's plight than the woman and Emma.

Emma tied off a vine and got up.

"Emma take to Mr. Mac's."

After Emma scooped up her coat and mittens, they left the sleeping patients and vigilant dogs. They marched to the other cabin taking time to plod a course through the mass of snow, and traverse the fallen tree, where an ominous trail of blood began snaking its way to another door. By the time they reached it, they were out of breath. Emma walked right in.

A similar cabin to the woman's and Emma's, there was a

divider separating a bed from the rest of the room. Ian could barely make out the furnishings in the light from the window.

"Mr. Mac?" Emma called into the room.

"Emma girl, how's Pearl?" The faint, troubled query filled the dark room.

Emma stepped forward and drew back the divider. "Ian here."

The look of calm suffering shifted to angst as the old man took in Ian's form.

"Who are you and what are you doing here?" he demanded.

"I'm Ian Campbell. I live on Waltham's Peak." He wanted to say he *owned* Waltham's Peak but thought better of it under the circumstances. "Emma has been coming to my house ever since I moved in. She hasn't come recently, so I grew concerned and came out to check on her. When I didn't find her, I followed her footsteps here." Ian knew there were all kinds of holes in his story. He hoped the man's condition would preclude a better explanation.

The man winced as he pulled himself into a sitting position. Emma automatically rearranged his pillows for him. Gently, she pulled the blankets to cover him. Ian shivered. He had been so focused on *whom* he would encounter, he hadn't considered *what* he would encounter. The room was warm enough, but not filled with warmth. This man was cold. Not to Emma, but to Ian. Had he not been hampered by his injury, Ian thought he would have been given the bum's rush by now.

Emma turned up a lantern, which had been burning faintly next to the bed. She lifted the blankets at the foot of the bed, drawing them back far enough to inspect the man's lower leg. Ian inadvertently drew in his breath. As Emma unwound a bandage from his leg, liquid red was released. Eventually, Ian could see bone. He was drawn to the bed by the severity of the injuries.

"Mister. You've got a bad injury here."

"I ain't daft, man!" The patient shouted through clenched teeth. The mere exertion of the shout caused him to lean back against his pillows. "I've got a compound fracture that's done

torn through the skin. It don't get any worse than that."
Clearly, the man was in agony. Had it been Ian under those
blankets, he wouldn't have handled the pain as well as this
man.

Emma moved about the cabin with familiarity. She tore
some strips from a blanket and laid three of them together,
refolding the unused portion, she set it near the stove. With
gentle, slow hands she deftly peeled off all the old bandages
and set them in a ready bowl.

Ian didn't know how to help, so he threw another log on
the fire in the wood stove. He came back to the bed and found
Emma reaching for the second strip of blanket while holding
the first in place. She motioned for Ian to hand her another
one. It was the last thing on the planet he wanted to do. He
handed her the strip and held the blankets out of her way.
When she had used up that strip, he gave her the last one,
neatly tying it off.

Ian was beginning to see why Emma was summoned. He'd
never spent much time around the sick. He hated hospitals. He
hated sickness. Even when Kat was sick, he had done what he
felt was required of a husband, but that was it. He knew Kat
understood that doctoring or nursing just wasn't his thing.

"Emma girl, thank you." The mountain man measured his
words beneath the pain. "You're an angel. No one coulda done
that any better or gentler than you just did. I'm mighty
grateful."

This girl was a saint. What moved Ian as he watched her
was her genuine concern. She cared about this mean old
mountain man. She cared about the old lady. She cared about
Pearl. That was why anyone would summon Emma. Who
wouldn't want to be cared for with such kind concern? Ian
straightened as the answer struck him. Ian. That's who. Ian
wouldn't want to be cared for. Emma had been coming to his
house for more than a month caring for him. And what had he
done? Everything he could to get rid of her.

"What are you doing here, Mr. Campbell? You just a casual
observer or you gonna help? Pearl needs a doctor. I don't

know what Emma told you, but she's had a high fever goin' on five days. I was on my way to get a doctor for her when that damn tree up and fell on me." The effort it took the man to relay his story was exhausting. He took a deep breath and continued. Ian was wondering if this guy wasn't some sort of savage saint. Was there such a thing?

"We've been working on a pallet for Pearl. I had it all done and ready to go when that tree took out me and the pallet. I was draggin' it over there when it happened. Can you believe them odds?"

Ian felt like he could believe it. After what he'd been through losing Kat and trying to lose Emma, he winced.

"It'd be hell on her to travel, but she's been unconscious for two days, so it may not be an issue. Besides, you don't have time to go get someone and come back. You just gotta get her down the mountain to help." He looked Ian in the eye. It was the first time he'd addressed him as an equal, as if Ian had some use.

That was it. That was the mission. The old man never said a word about himself. Ian considered the project on the floor in the cabin next door. That must have been the pallet of which the old man had spoken.

"Look, Mr. ..."

"McLean, the name's Hamish McLean." Understanding dawned.

"Look, Mr. MacLean, I'd love to help, but I'm no mountain man. If I start traipsing around these woods in the dark I may end up in West Virginia. I barely got myself here and you're only a couple miles from my place."

MacLean lost the useful look. Ian had just been demoted in the eyes of the mountain man.

"You take one of the dogs. They know their way around. Emma goes to town once or twice a month and always has 'em with her. You tell Pax you're headin' to Ol' Smith's to get Emma's hair cut and he'll get you there." He was tiring fast. MacLean squeezed his eyes shut and sucked in raspy breaths, apparently willing his thoughts to stay focused.

Emma had been in the background washing soiled linens with boiling water on the stove. Efficiency was her strong suit as long as she knew her way around a place. She stepped outside long enough to dispose of the dirty water, and finished cleaning the rags and pans, hanging the linens by the fire in the time it took MacLean to explain the rescue process to Ian. Now she was putting some leftover stew on the stove to warm, presumably for MacLean's supper.

The room was darker now than it had been when Ian first stepped in. He gauged it was about 1:30. If he waited much longer, he would never make it down the mountain before dark. It was now or never.

"I'll send help," he muttered.

The mountain man raised himself on one elbow and shouted at Ian's receding figure, "We don't have time for that! Damn you! Don't you see? It's now or never! You have got to get that girl down this mountain!"

Pulling the door open and facing the empty expanse before him, Ian repeated, "I'll send help."

Chapter 16

WEIGHT OF THE WORLD

"Ian, just meet me for lunch one day at the hospital." Ian and Kat chatted between bites of Ian's specialty salmon, which lay on the dinner table between them. "The kids are precious. After all the stories I've told about you, little Trina has been asking to meet you. And Roger wants your autograph. I promise to buy you a cape if you agree to come." Kat grinned her most mischievous grin.

The last place in the universe Ian wanted to be was a hospital. "Kat, what is it with these sick kids? Isn't it depressing hanging out with them knowing they might not make it?"

Kat lost the grin and gained her sober look. "Should I only visit kids who are healthy, Ian? Kids who have friends, homework and sports to keep them busy?"

"Well, it'd be a hell of a better investment of your time and a lot less detrimental to your psyche. Besides, you can go get a manicure or play tennis at the club. Why spend your time with those kids?" Ian was spitting out the words as he finished his argument.

Kat finished chewing. He watched her pause to take a sip of wine, wiping her mouth with the linen napkin he had placed under her fork. She leaned both arms on the table, gazed at him, and carefully smiled. From somewhere very far away, he heard her say, "If I can't have my own child, Ian, I might as well bless someone who's losing theirs."

Emma and MacLean looked up to see Ian's haggard frame silhouetted against the door. It had been a long five minutes since he had walked out the door; an eternity of memory and regret. Ian heard himself asking a question.

"OK, MacLean. Can you tell a city slicker how to get a sick girl down a mountain covered in four feet of snow with just a dog and a backpack?"

Thirty minutes later, Ian was fed and packed. The stew had been for them both: the logging mountain man and the retired defense attorney. Emma was smarter than he thought. The pallet had been completed when Ian watched Emma pull the last vine through and fasten it to the branches.

With tremendous care, Ian and Emma carried their young patient cocooned in quilts to the pallet. A now watchful Ruby silently assisted with all the preparations. She hadn't said a word to Ian beyond, "My pack's ready." He didn't bother to argue in spite of her tired, old frame. MacLean had assured her that Ruby could make the trip. She'd even be an asset, he said.

A tarp was laid over the entire rig to keep the snow from melting down into the warm layers atop Pearl's body. Pax was leashed to Ian and Ruby was tethered to the pallet, lest snow flurries separate any one from the others. As they stepped out of the cabin, Ian and Ruby both knelt to affix their snowshoes. Pax, the even-tempered hound that he was, calmly stood at attention, seemingly knowledgeable of the task before him.

"You'll be going downhill, remember," MacLean had advised, "so gravity will be helping you along. Ruby hasn't made the trip in a long while, but she'll remember. Between the dog and the grandmother, you'll make it. I know it sounds crazy, Mr. Campbell, but I have a suspicion that Pearl has Scarlet Fever." He let that sink in.

"If that's so, Mr. Campbell, that rash you see on Ruby is just the beginning for her, too. She's probably already feeling it, just not sayin' so."

Ian felt his Adam's apple jolt. He hadn't signed up for this. An epidemic disease that killed thousands before it was penicillined out in the 1940s was going to be following him down a mountain for the next several hours. He didn't dare open his mouth for fear fear would come out of it. After all, if he didn't do this, Emma would.

He put one foot in front of the other and found a makeshift hospital gurney and a sick old woman following in his footsteps. The dog was ahead of him resolutely moving down the mountain. As her goodbye, Emma had gently taken Pax's head in her hands, looked him in the eye and said, "Ol' Smith's, Pax. Take Pearl to Ol' Smith's."

Ian wished she'd given the key words "clinic" or "doctor," something more useful or closer in proximity to what he needed. The barbershop was a good distance from the only clinic in town and Ian wasn't sure he knew how to make up the difference from this direction. He longed for a Garmon to tell him, "recomputing."

About an hour into the trek, Ruby began slowing. He consistently had to tell Pax to wait or slow down. Finally, he crossed paths with his own prints from earlier in the morning. He breathed a sigh of relief. At least they were moving in the right direction. Just as he exhaled, he saw Ruby go down.

She fell next to the pallet, her hand extended toward it. In spite of the fact that she was face down in the freezing snow, her body didn't move. That was all Ian needed to know his situation had just gone from bad to worse. Setting down the pallet, Ian made his way over to her prone body and rolled her over.

"Ruby. Ruby!" He yelled into her face. Her eyes fluttered open and shut again. He was close enough to her to know that she was burning up. Her face was red and her breathing shallow. He let go of her and fell back in the snow.

"Aaaaaahhhhhhhh!" he roared. "Why? Why am I on my mountain with a dog that's not mine, a kid who's got an extinct disease, and a guide who's unconscious? What's wrong with this picture!" His body came off the snow as he raged on, propelled by his anger.

"I can't find my wife, but I can find people that don't exist! God, why is this happening to me?" Ian pulled himself into a crouching position. He was tired. He hadn't realized how tired until just now. He had spent the day before chopping wood, when the most weight he was used to pushing around was the letter "i" on his keyboard. The most cutting and chopping he did took place with his Misono Gyutou and a zucchini. And now he'd spent the last six hours trekking through knee-deep snow rescuing sick people.

He grabbed the pack and slung it around his body. Pushing Ruby up against the pallet, he considered his own condition. He needed a drink and some grub. Perhaps he was getting delirious from dehydration. He gulped some water and downed a granola bar and apple. After surveying the landscape, he took note of the placement of the sun, comparing it to his notes. If he was right, his house was about a half hour southeast of his current location. Glancing over at Pax resting in the snow, Ian found fortitude. With a satisfied stomach, he felt a little more clear-headed.

Crouching, Ian embraced Ruby and lifted her with a grunt. Tired as he was, it felt like he was carrying the world. He had to stop every few minutes to shift Ruby's weight. Eventually, he draped her over his shoulder in the fireman's carry, supporting Ruby with one hand while dragging Pearl's pallet with the other.

When he finally emerged from the tree line and saw Uplands in the distance, Ian stopped for a breath. He didn't put anything down lest he lack the energy to pick it up again.

With painstaking lethargy, Ian made his way to Uplands with his burdens. The pallet he left at the bottom of the stairs as he took Ruby inside. He took her upstairs and laid her down on the guest room bed. Feeling light after having carried her so long, he had renewed energy.

Pax was seated beside the pallet when Ian returned. With an uncharacteristic gentleness, Ian unwrapped the tarp and wriggled his fingers under Pearl's listless frame. With Pax by his side, he carried Pearl to the same room and placed her in bed beside her grandmother. He had reasoned that in the unlikely event that either of them awoke while he was gone, they would be reassured in their strange surroundings by seeing the other.

Food and water for Pax was presented in Campbell plaid china on the kitchen floor. He made himself a quart of coffee, thermosed it, ate another bar, and set out again with Pax beside him.

"Ol' Smith's, Pax. Let's get our hair cut."

Taking a bearing of south southeast, Ian exerted full confidence in the dog, little in himself. Every step of the downward journey, Pax had been ahead of him. Even when they changed directions at the crossroads, Pax had taken the lead. The dog was a canine compass.

A sense of vigor that Ian had not previously experienced came over him. He attributed it to the coffee and the calories. Ridding himself of so many burdens had made a difference, too, no doubt. He was virtually jogging down the mountain keeping pace with Pax as they cleared the tree line and spied lights winking in the distance.

The sun was setting twice as fast as usual with every step he took down the east side of his peak. He located the headlamp in his pack and kept walking. An hour later, he found himself careening down an escarpment where SR129 dumped him out at the Tasty—eeze.

What good fortune. This wasn't where he had expected to end up. He had assumed he and Pax would head straight for the barber's, instead, they found themselves a half mile from the clinic. Not a car was in sight. The road had been plowed, but was again impassable. Other businesses up and down the road were closed and empty. This was no place to be after a snowstorm the Friday night before Christmas.

Flakes began fluttering before his eyes. Apparently the snow hadn't finished falling. He picked up the pace and headed toward the clinic. Although it was snowed in too, lights were on and footprints abounded in the area prefacing the front door. He held the door for Pax and leaned against the wall in the foyer to take off his snowshoes.

Entering with dog in tow, Ian noted the emergency lights were on. Everything else was still and silent. He hollered a "hello."

"I'll be right with you!" was released from a room in the back of the building. Ian walked toward it.

"I'll be right with *you*," Ian returned. He rounded the corner and there was Patty.

"Sir, we'll be right with you. We have a patient right now and ..." Ian didn't let her finish.

"Listen, I'm sorry to interrupt you, but I have an emergency." He briefly explained to her what the situation was. As he listened to himself talk, he felt that he wasn't making any sense at all. Inwardly, he was worried that his incoherence was going to impede his plan somehow.

"Am I making any sense, Patty?" he appealed to her.

"Yes, sir. I think you're telling me that you've got some Scarlet Fever cases at your house up the mountain."

"That's it, Patty. I've got to take a doctor back with me. The child has been deathly ill for five days now and she and her grandmother are both unconscious at my house."

"But, sir, we're ..." Patty looked apologetic.

"I'll go."

Patty and Ian both turned to see Curly Doc standing in the hallway pulling gloves off her hands. Her headlamp illuminated her hands as she worked.

"If what you say is true, Mr. Campbell, the child is in grave danger." She reached up and turned off the lamp. Addressing them both she announced, "Patty, I've gotten the patient stitched. They'll need to be cleaned and advised as to directions for care. I've already written the script, so they're good to go. Dr. Preston is scheduled to be here for the night shift. I think you can hold down the fort until then."

"Doc, you haven't slept since ..." Patty began again.

"I'll be fine, Patty." She looked at Ian and asked, "How did you get here with 129 blocked?"

"We walked." At this, Pax ambled up and sat down next to

him. Ian rested his hand on Pax's head in thanks. He felt like explaining what he'd done that day and get a rush from their looks of awe. Somehow he knew that would diminish whatever sense of purpose or goodness had come out of this day. Instead, he proceeded with his course of action. "Do you have snowshoes here, Doc, or some other means of keeping yourself above the snow?"

"I sure do." She marched past Pax, whose appearance in the clinic didn't seem to matter when the town was functioning on emergency lighting. Ian and Pax followed as Patty made her way back to the waiting patient.

Curly Doc turned on her headlamp as she rummaged in the darkness behind the front desk. She bent into the recesses of the cupboard and emerged with a keychain. The keychain only had one key on it.

"Snowshoes on steroids," she said as she held up her find.

BETSY BOYD LESLIE

Chapter 17

HOSPITAL..ITY

Figuring out how to get the pack, medical supplies, snowshoes and poles on the back of the snowmobile was one thing. Getting Pax on it was another.

"Listen Campbell, no offense, but I think I'm going to have to drive while you hold the horse. He's not going to stay on by himself and I can't hold him. He weighs more than I do!"

He could barely hear her muffled ideas through the layers of hats and scarves she was wearing. The snow was falling pretty steadily now and they needed to get going. Time was of the essence. Even Doc had said so. She could see he wasn't going for her latest idea.

"Will he run alongside?" She was doubtful but hopeful.

"I don't want to risk it. He might run back to Emma and then I'd have a hard time finding my house again with the new snowfall. I need him to help navigate if we get lost. Besides, he's done a lot of work today. I doubt he'd make it at a run."

"I've got one other idea. You do know how to drive one of these things, right?"

Ian wasn't sure. He'd driven one, but not *this* one. He was looking down at what was emblazoned ASSAULT. The Assault was twenty years old if a day. All of the gas in the storage area had been drained into the tank. He wondered if it took leaded. He had doubted it worked until she sat astride it, turned the key and heard it roar into life. Clearly, made in America used to mean something.

"What's your idea this time, Doc? I'm fresh out." He felt so very tired. If they didn't start moving soon, he'd have to find a warm place to take a nap. On second thought, it didn't even have to be warm.

He didn't like the idea, but he had to agree. For his own sake, if not the inert bodies in his house, or the mountain man with the compound fracture, he had to get moving.

With Ian at the helm, Pax in the seat behind him, and Curly Doc straddling the baggage compartment, they began their tenuous journey home. Ian found himself calling it "home" as he drove toward it. He'd always referred to it as Uplands either when talking to others or thinking to himself. He'd spent countless hours creating it, so up until now it had been a creation, a habitation, not a home.

The snowmobile began sputtering as they went over a particularly steep rise. He maneuvered it to run parallel with the mountain in order to give it a rest. For the next few minutes the machine caught its breath. Curly Doc used the time to rest her arms and reposition Pax.

They reached the house without further incident, but it took twice as long as the trek down. Ian had to keep stopping to get his bearings, and the snowmobile needed periodic rests. Ian had to put both his headlamp and Doc's on in order to maintain a visual. The persistent precipitation didn't help either.

He pulled into the other bay of his carport. After helping Pax dismount, he grabbed the medical equipment Doc wasn't carrying and headed to the mudroom door. It was quiet enough inside to assume that no one stirred. Ian lighted a lantern and took Doc upstairs. Both patients lay exactly as he'd left them. The stillness was ominous.

Headlamp on, Doc immediately set to checking pulses. After ensuring that both patients were still alive, she issued a few orders to Ian.

His first task was to get a raging fire going and take the chill off the house. He was glad for all the hard work he'd put in the day before. Was that just yesterday? Chopping wood seemed like a distant memory. After lugging in lumber, inserting his magic lighter knot and striking a match, he had a fire going that would do any Boy Scout proud. He pulled down a discrete glass door and flicked a switch. In no time at all, the heat radiating from this fire would be funneled all over the house.

He'd spent an entire Thanksgiving figuring out how to employ this functional feature in his home without the unsightly bells and whistles. He wanted to pat himself on the back for yet another great result of his efforts. Like the feeling he'd had back at the clinic, somehow the gesture, albeit a mental one, didn't seem right today. Ignoring his fatigue, he set about boiling water, warming broth, fetching towels, and completing the other needs on the Doc's list.

The next time he returned to the guest room, both patients had been stripped and sponged. Blankets lay over them both while Ian collected their soiled laundry.

"Do you have anything that would remotely fit them?" Doc asked.

Ian sized up the woman and child, a formality really, since he could almost tell to the ounce how much they each weighed after today.

"Kat, my wife, has a closet full of clothes here. I'll see what I can find." He hurried off, throwing the soiled laundry in the washer on the way. They emitted a mixture of piney freshness and stagnant soil but mostly just fevered sickness. Just as he was about to toss in some detergent he recalled the lack of power to his machine.

"Would sweats work?" Ian asked as he made his way back into the room. "They'd be the easiest to get on them and the simplest fitting."

"Great idea," Doc asserted as she placed her thermometer on the table and took the sweats from him.

"What kind of temperature are they running?"

"Both above one oh five. You were right. It's Scarlet Fever."

I gave them each injections of antibiotics and am keeping close track of their temperatures. I need to monitor that and the injections closely. This is a severe case with the child having had such a high fever for so long. The fact that the grandmother has it is troubling, since it's uncommon in someone her age. It may even be an especially virulent strain to have shown up when and how it did. Something tells me this is going to be a long night." She brushed a curl away from her face and clutched the sweats to her. As she took in their faces, she asked, "So, how did you end up with two gems in your guest room?"

"It wasn't easy. I'll tell you sometime when we have fewer emergencies on our hands. Once I bring up the tea and water will you be needing anything else?"

"Yeah," she listed a few items.

"Perfect, be back in five with the goods."

Downstairs, Ian pulled out a tray and began filling it. As he waited for the water to boil again, he made several trips out the mudroom door until the hearth had sufficient firewood to last into the morning. Stepping over the sleeping dog didn't bother him for a change. He stirred the embers and piled on several logs. Tea, water, bowls, cups, spoons, straws, towels, and a cup of coffee for the Doc, were assembled with nurse-like efficiency.

He padded up the stairs and set the tray next to Doc who was taking blood pressures. He quietly slipped out. Although the house had finally reached a mildly comfortable fifty degrees, he noticed the Doc had goose bumps. Once she'd taken off her parka, her long-sleeved scrubs were not a sufficient barrier to the indoor cold.

He rummaged through Kat's things looking for a light jacket or sweater that would fit Doc. An unexpected pang arrested him. He missed Kat. Her face came into full and sudden view. He missed his wife. Were she here, she would be a good and gentle nurse. She would have given the mountain man a pleasant smile and careful touch. She wouldn't have resented their presence or needs. She would have been all that Ian wasn't.

He had never appreciated who Kat was. What had initially drawn him to her – gentleness, kindness, goodness – he had eventually perceived as weakness. Ian eschewed anything weak. Succumbing to the longing for her strength, he grabbed a velour green jacket Kat loved to wear around Uplands, buried his face in her scent, and wept.

BETSY BOYD LESLIE

Chapter 18

OUT OF AFRICA

Thrusting a jeans jacket at Doc, he smiled. "Thanks for putting in some overtime on your Christmas vacation." She smiled a weary smile and took the jacket.

"You won't be thanking me when you get the bill." She put on the jacket and sipped her coffee. She noticed Ian's red, bloodshot eyes, chalking it up to wind and fatigue.

"However, I will deduct this cup of coffee from it. This is probably the best cup of coffee I have had on three continents. How did you manage it?"

"French press. It's the only way to go and it doesn't require a power source other than me."

He leaned over the bed and took in the shapes before him. Although they were both still unconscious, they now looked more like they were asleep. Something had changed in their countenance. Just as importantly, Ian noticed, they were both now clean and dressed in Kat's sweats. Just looking at their changed conditions improved Ian's mood. Maybe they'd be okay after all. After his effort.

"How old do you think she is?"

"About sixty."

"No, the child. How old is Pearl?"

"Well, I'm not an expert in pediatrics, but judging by her teeth and size, I'd say she's about seven, give or take a year."

"Is she going to make it?"

"I don't know. Had we gotten those antibiotics in her any later, I wouldn't even be that optimistic."

Leaning against the wall Ian asked what the next twelve hours looked like.

"They'll probably continue to sleep. In the morning I'm going to try to get some liquids in them, but it will probably be more of this," she waved her free hand toward the sleeping patients, "for some time."

"I've got the fire built up, so it should last a while." Motioning toward a door behind the Doc, Ian added, "Through the bathroom is another room with a really comfortable couch. I bought it specifically for its sleeping potential. I've thrown some blankets and extra pillows in there for you. You can shower and freshen up, 'cause the hot water heater is gas, not electric. If you'd prefer to sleep in here, I can rig something up for you." He started walking toward the door and looked back.

"I couldn't ask for more, Ian, thank you. You've thought of everything."

"You could have asked for a night off. Oh, yeah, I've also assembled a pile of clothes for you out of Kat's things. They should fit, you're similar sizes, and the things I chose are relaxed fit, anyway."

"Thank you again, in spite of the 'relaxed fit' comment. I think I'll take you up on your couch offer as soon as I wrap some things up here." She paused and set her coffee mug on the tray. "I don't know when the last time was that you heard the news, but we're in for more snow for the next two to three days. There's no telling when these roads will be cleared."

"I can tell you when they're getting cleared," Ian offered. "According to the state road maintenance office, they aren't on the agenda until next week. I have some ideas before we get to that point, but for now, I just want to focus on the next twelve hours." He turned to go. "Need anything else, Doc?"

"No, why don't you get a good night sleep. I'll call you if I need anything."

"Sleep?" Ian looked weary, but resolved, "No, not yet. I have one more patient to fetch."

Ian stepped out of the room and headed for the stairs. Doc followed him and quizzed him from the landing.

"Is this next one the reason I had to bring the fracture kit?"

"Yep," he called from below, "and you may need to use it on more than one of us if that snowmobile doesn't cooperate."

Downstairs, Ian double-checked his pack contents. He refilled his water bottle, threw in an emergency blanket, added the Doc's headlamp, and summoned Pax. As he placed his hand on the doorknob, he noticed the Doc behind him.

"When did you sleep last, Ian?"

"I got a full eight hours last night, Doc. I've only been up since six." He stood with his back to the door, taking in her tired visage. "I've probably had the same amount of sleep or less than you."

"Are you sure you don't want to wait until morning? As it is, you may not get back until two or three in the morning. If you get lost, fall off the mountain, or experience a setback of any kind, you may not make it back until tomorrow. There's no shame in waiting until daylight, Ian."

He set down his pack to spare even that energy. Pausing before he spoke, he asked, "Doc, how long does it take for sepsis to set in when there's exposed bone?"

She stood arms akimbo as she delivered the information. "Depending on the conditions and environment in which the break occurred, it could set in immediately, in which case symptoms could develop in twelve to thirty-six hours."

"Doc, this man set out three days ago to bring that little girl to you when he had his accident. He's in a cabin with no electricity and no medicine. He needs to get to a hospital yesterday." Ian looked down at the hardwood floors, an unfinished thought hanging in the air.

"For the first time in forty years, I've done something that mattered. You may not understand, since you've lived a life of

worthwhile activity. I'm on a roll, Doc, and I can't stop now."
He picked up his pack, scrubbed Pax's head and moved to the
door. "Be back in five with the goods."

Pax followed Ian out to the snowmobile. While Ian
fastened the pallet on to the baggage compartment, Pax fixed
him with a stare. Finally, Ian jockeyed into position behind the
handlebars.

"Come on, boy, it's just you and me, so we're going to have
to get cozy." Pax peered up at him with doleful eyes. He didn't
move. Ian patted the seat in front of him. Pax didn't budge.
Ian got off the machine and patted his leg.

"Come on, Pax, let's figure this out." After ten minutes of
heaving and hefting, Ian sat against the snowmobile staring at
the dog seated in the snow.

"Just when I was beginning to like you. Look, Pax, we've
got to get back to Emma. She's ..." Ian was transfixed as he
watched the dog's retreating shape. At the mention of Emma's
name, Pax sensed permission. Ian jumped astride the
ASSAULT to catch up to the jogging figure.

By the time he had the aged machine fired up and moving
in the right direction, Pax was a good quarter mile ahead of
him with a bearing of north by northwest. Pax wasn't headed
to Emma's house, he was headed to the old man's. "Smart
dog," thought Ian.

An hour and a half later, Ian stopped his engine outside the
old man's door. Pax stood at the entrance, silently entreating to
go in. Emma opened the door.

"Mr. Mac in bad shape."

Ian didn't have time to catch his breath before the next
assault. He walked over to the bed where MacLean was
feverishly tossing and turning. The blankets and quilts were red
with blood loss. A stench was beginning to form in the room.

"Emma, get ready to go, we're leaving now."

Obediently, Emma began dressing for the outdoors. Ian

retrieved the pallet and prepared it for another chrysalis. As gently as possible, he and Emma wrapped MacLean in his quilts, making sure to pin his arms to his body in the swaddling process. Ian couldn't help but wince and gag as they wrapped the infected leg and he felt the bones give against the pressure.

When MacLean's body was ready, they carried him to the pallet. Again, Ian covered his body and quilts with the tarp. He grabbed a coil of rope he'd seen against the cabin and dragged the pallet out to the snowmobile. While Emma watered Pax and thanked him for his good work, Ian secured the pallet to the Assault. When he was certain of his knots, he hailed Emma.

"Emma, I want you to sit on this seat and watch the pallet, okay?" She stared at him.

He got on the seat facing backward and spoke to her. "You will sit like this. If anything goes wrong, you jab me in the ribs with your elbow and I'll stop, okay?"

Emma continued to stare, wide-eyed.

"Emma, have you ever ridden one of these before?"

"Nope." Ian didn't have time for this. Like Kat used to say, there was no way around it, but through it.

"You sit on it like a chair, Emma. It makes noise and moves, but it's just a chair."

She stared some more.

"Have you sat in Mr. Mac's rocking chair, Emma?"

"Yes, Emma like to rock."

"Well, this is like that but faster. If you'll sit with me we can get Mr. Mac to help. He needs medicine, Emma, and this will help us get him there fast."

Emma stepped toward the machine. Ian could tell she was terrified, and was impressed with her courage. Just like Pax moved at the mention of his beloved's name, so did Emma at the word "help."

She clumsily got on the machine with Ian's steadying hand. Glancing back at MacLean occasionally, he finished getting Emma and himself settled and rechecked the knots. With a furtive roar, the engine came to life. Emma jumped, but stayed in position. As an afterthought, Ian unwrapped Doc's headlamp from his head and put it on Emma.

"We're gonna move now, Emma, hold on to the seat."

"Pax, Rex, come on. Let's go to Grampa's." Both dogs came to attention and strode in the direction of Ian's house. Ian carefully throttled the engine and they were off. It was so dark and the snow had covered so much of his previous trail, that Ian found himself following the dogs. He aimed his headlamp at their flagging tails and mechanically steered after them.

When they came to a stand of trees, through which their trail lead, the Assault began sputtering. With a dull throb and hesitating lurch, the engine cut off entirely. Ian tried cranking the engine, to no avail.

"Damn!" Ian bashed the handlebars in frustration.

"Empty," offered Emma. Sure enough, the gas gauge was pointing to a thick red line.

Emma hopped off the machine. Pax and Rex were at her side in a moment. She began unwinding the ropes and undoing the knots which secured the pallet. Ian watched. She wasn't getting very far and had to remove her mittens. Ian knew her fingers were freezing working against the metal. He grabbed his pack and removed a knife. With four quick jerks, the pallet was freed from the snowmobile. MacLean stirred restlessly.

They had only the tree stand before them and then a half mile down to Uplands. Thankfully, the gas had gotten them this far. Ian wasn't sure he could have gone any further on foot than what lay ahead. He was bone weary.

Again, he found himself marching mechanically in the wake of the dogs. He'd never trusted anyone, let alone a dog, like he trusted them now. This going was far more challenging, since he'd left the snowshoes at Uplands. Slogging through the snow, creating deep fissures in the path and deeper fissures in the drifts, was laborious and draining. The pallet, a makeshift assemblage of vines, arrested any forward movement and fought him with every step. In his fatigue, the trek became a matter of mind over body. He willed himself to take a step, stop, pull, take another step and pull. The chill was beginning to seep through his pants where the snow found its way above his boots. His fingers, in spite of the gloves, were aching, the tips gone cold long ago as they'd gripped the handles of the Assault. Flurries continued to strike his cheeks, numbing his nose, searing his ears.

They approached the tree line, noting a weak light in the house in the distance. In spite of the finish line before him, he simply had to rest. He asked Emma to stop for a moment, while he scraped the snow off a nearby boulder and collapsed against it. MacLean, like his last two patients, remained asleep or unconscious. He didn't know which.

Emma watched him and held out her hand.

"I pull Mr. Mac." Her bundled face was sincere, her gesture more than a gesture.

"No, I've got it, Emma. I just needed a short rest." He stood and steadied himself. As resolute and unselfish as she was, Ian knew she lacked the strength to pull the dead weight of MacLean against the draw of the snow.

"I told Doc I'd be back in five, so let's get going."

Ian didn't recall the last half-mile. He found himself standing before his stairs and Emma unwrapping MacLean. He couldn't bear MacLean alone, but somewhere in the arrival, Doc appeared. Among the three of them, they were able to get MacLean to Ian's couch before the hearth.

"Doc, what do you need?" Ian heard himself say. The mere fact that he had achieved his objective with the warmth of his fire seeping into his frame, gave him renewed energy. She was crouching over MacLean's form, peeling away the layers of quilt, clothing and bandaging. Emma stood at his feet, watching with rapt attention.

"Who did this bandaging?" Doc asked.

"Emma bandage Mr. Mac." Emma's earnest eyes shifted from Mac to Doc. Ian volunteered to translate.

"Doc meet Emma. Emma, meet Doctor Laura Tate." The Doc looked Emma square in the eye as she held the bandages aloft.

"You did this Emma? You took care of this man?"

"Yes, Emma help."

"You did a fine job. He's probably alive because of you, Emma." She smiled at her and Emma quickly did the same.

"We have a lot of work ahead of us." She dropped the bandages into the pile of soiled clothing and quilts, wrapping them so that the worst of the discharge was covered.

"Ian, I know you're tired, but I'm going to need you just a little bit longer. Can you last another hour?"

"You got it, Doc." He made his way to the kitchen and noticed that water was already boiling. Doc must have been watching for their return and prepared a few things in anticipation of their needs. It was she who had lighted a lamp and placed it in the kitchen window, heralding their way home. He hadn't thought that far ahead when he left. He was glad she had. In place by the couch, he had noticed sheets, towels, bandages and other items she'd set out in anticipation of a triage patient.

Ian peered at the ticking grandfather clock and noted the time. It was five thirty. No wonder he was tired; he had been up almost twenty-four hours straight. He did not even want to think how many miles he had covered in that time.

As he prepared himself and his medical team hot coffee, he noticed another pile of supplies in the kitchen. Doc must have really rooted around to find these items. Among them was a one hundred year-old bottle of brandy. It was unopened. He reached out to retrieve the brandy bottle and return it to its rightful location. It was more than brandy; it was *the* brandy. Brandy he'd spent an entire retainer on. Brandy he and Kat were supposed to share to celebrate their retirement in Uplands.

He heard Doc giving Emma some careful instructions, which Emma was setting to with a will. Watching Emma work without question, without complaint, unhesitatingly responding to Doc's requests was bracing.

He remembered the tarp and went outside to retrieve it leaving the brandy bottle where Doc had placed it. With Doc off sanitizing knives and preparing sutures, he covered the

Persian rug under the couch. He watched the expression on MacLean's face to see if it changed as Ian shuffled around him. MacLean was in another world; no noises, no movements affected him any longer.

Doc reappeared carrying Ian's straightedge razor, and his special order, deep pocket, 350 count Egyptian ecru cotton sheets.

"Ian, you've got a nice place and real nice accoutrements. I can tell you're not a Target customer. As a matter of fact, I wouldn't know where to get some of this finery. I just know it is. Tell me when I cross a line. I will make do with whatever you allow me to use. In Africa I did far more with far less."

She walked over to her pile of supplies he'd seen in the kitchen. Adding her new pieces and picking them all up, she put them on the coffee table next to MacLean and spread them out in surgical room fashion.

"My plan is to set the fracture the best I can and shoot him up with a bunch of penicillin. I brought enough to cure an army. After setting the bone, I'll need to stitch a few things back together and then secure it with some kind of splint. This should hold him until the cavalry arrives. The whole procedure will take me between one and two hours. I'll need you and Emma for the first hour to help me hold him down and put the splint in place. Can you do that?"

"You haven't even seen my resume yet and I'm already hired? Was it my sense of humor or taste in bath towels that sold you?"

"Great, then here's what we still need and then we can get started. First, look at these things. Are you willing to let me use them?" She met Ian's weary gaze with her earnest query.

Ian again resisted the urge to reclaim his brandy. He had mixed emotions about the sheets and so many other things, but was overcome with shame when he considered how MacLean had gotten injured to begin with, when he considered Emma's altruistic efforts over the last week, when he thought of these people willing to put each other first at every turn of the emergency.

"Perfect. I've been waiting for just the right surgical moment to break out my vintage brandy. You've done me a favor, Doc!" He smiled and sat back cupping his coffee.

Chapter 19

CLINICAL TRIALS

Kat's hair had fallen out of the ponytail she'd made the morning before. Her linen blouse had more wrinkles than he knew linen could hold. Bloodshot eyes and smeared mascara told Ian she'd done more than stay up all night. She'd been crying. A lot. She now slumped over the side of the bed trying to undress, hampered by her tears.

"For god's sake, Kat," Ian sat up on his side of the bed and picked up his clock for a closer look. "It's two in the morning. You've been with that kid all this time?"

She didn't turn. She didn't move. She spoke into her lap. "Roger didn't make it, Ian. He came out of surgery just fine, then this afternoon his body started rejecting the new bone marrow." She could no longer stem the sobs. They came freely and deeply. Ian leaned forward and rubbed her back.

"The doctors said they had never seen a more rapid rejection. He's gone, Ian. He's gone. That poor, dear family lost their boy." She fell over against the pillows and quietly wept under her tangle of hair.

Ian lay next to her holding her as she cried. "Kat, you've got to stop this. You can be a classroom aid or volunteer at the symphony. You won't wear yourself out like this."

Kat's sobs slowed as she turned and looked Ian full in the face. "When people are hurting, Ian, is when help is needed most and the hardest to find."

"Let's finish the prep work and get this show on the road."
Doc explained how the splint would need to be applied and
Ian set to work finding the right materials. He came back with
duct tape, monogrammed hand towels, a Scottish linen
tablecloth he'd picked out on their honeymoon, a three-foot
garden tool, a rake handle and his firehawk.

"The next time I place an order with my medical supplies
company, I'm going to ask them to throw in one of these!" She
held up the firehawk in open admiration.

"You should see it in action. This little deelywhop here," he
put his mouth on the flange at the top end, "is for blowing on the
fire without singeing your eyebrows." He blew to make his point.

"I gathered that, but the demonstration was helpful. You
should have been in sales. If the surgeon thing doesn't work
out, you may want to consider it." She worked and talked.

While Ian relaxed into the warm luxury of his chair, Doc
strode to the kitchen sink where she washed her face and arms
thoroughly. Ian figured some of it was for sanitation, but also
wakefulness. She hadn't slept in two days either. For that
matter, how much had Emma slept? Sleep deprivation was as
contagious as the fever.

As the sun came up the lanterns and headlamps gradually
lost their effectiveness. The clock struck six. Ian considered
Doc's ablutions, then ran upstairs and repeated the same
procedure he'd just watched her perform. He poked his head
in sickbay and saw Emma seated where Doc had been. She was
reaching for the cloth on Pearl's forehead as Ian stepped in.

"How's she doing, Emma?" Ian asked.

"Pearl still hot." She replaced the cloth and sat back.

"We're going to have Mr. Mac taken care of soon, Emma.
We're going to need your help. You've done so much already
that I hate to ask. He will want to see your pretty face if he
wakes up, so we want you there to help us hold him still,
okay?"

"Emma help. Mr. Mac friend." She quickly gave up her
rocking chair and started downstairs.

Emma unhesitatingly approached MacLean's face, looking for any signs of recognition, but was greeted by the same slumber she'd left him in. Doc made the universal symbol for surgical preparedness. Her hands were positioned straight up in the air adorned by yellow latex kitchen gloves. As Ian took in the patient, he noticed that the area around the fracture had been washed, shaved and brandied.

"For now, Emma, you stay at Mr. MacLean's head and hold his hands just like you're doing now. If he wakes up, you just say something to him so that he knows you're here. That will calm him down faster than anything, I think." Emma nodded in understanding.

"Ian, I'm going to need you to pull the foot of his injured leg as hard as you can until I say, 'done.' What you're doing is pulling the bone back down against the draw of the muscles and tendons, so that it gives me some leeway to fit the bone back in place. The good news is I think it was a clean break with no shards or splinters involved. The bad news is that it is at a very bad angle for fixing on a living room couch, in spite of the fact that it's a Bugatti." Ian wondered yet again at her attention to detail. If she spent so long in the wilds of Africa, how did she know a $9000 couch when she saw one?

"You'll get on your knees and pull straight back, trying to correct the angle it's at now. I will try to put the bone back into position while you are pulling. So, when I say, 'pull,' you pull his leg away from his body, trying to stay parallel with the upper part of his leg. Got it?"

"I think so. I'm the puller, you're the pusher. I start when you say, 'pull,' I stop when you say, 'done.'"

"That's it." She turned to look at Emma.

"Emma, this is a painful procedure. If he wakes up, you need to know he'll be in a lot of pain. I'm sorry, but there's nothing I can do about that. I've already given him the only painkiller I have, but it won't be enough. So, if he wakes up and screams, don't be frightened, okay? We'll take care of him. Do you understand?"

Doc's face asked the question as much as her intonation

did. Ian didn't know what would happen, but he trusted this curly Doc. He also trusted Emma.

"Doc help Mr. Mac. Emma help Doc." Her trusting nature touched Ian.

"Before we begin, I want to say a quick word of prayer." Before Ian could comment or object, Doc had begun, "Heavenly Father, we thank you for the life of Mr. MacLean. We thank you for Emma's superb care of him at his home. We thank you for Ian risking his own life to bring him here. We pray your blessing on these individuals. I pray that you would guide my hands as I do this thing. Protect him, heal him, help us. In the name of your Son, Jesus, we pray. Amen."

With that, Doc turned on her headlamp, stuck her hand into MacLean's leg and the surgery began.

Ian rolled over and squinted at the grandfather clock. The peal of the strike still rang through his head. He picked up his Cvstos chronograph next to the hearth and read the time. Something familiar, yet unexpected, struck his senses: bacon and eggs. He tried turning on the nearby lamp, only to be reminded that the power was out. Rolling over with the watch, he held it out to a ray of sunshine. It was 1:00 p.m. Perhaps the solitary strike of the clock had awakened him.

He was still dressed in yesterday's clothes, so he undressed and showered. Exhaustion still overwhelmed him. His muscles ached and his head throbbed. After pulling on some clean clothes and combing his hair, he walked downstairs. He didn't bother to peer in sickbay for fear he'd wake someone. Pax and Rex were splayed at the bottom of the stairs, motionless from yesterday's activity.

"I know how you feel," muttered Ian as he stepped over them.

In the kitchen, he found Emma scraping eggs onto a plate. She acknowledged him with a smile. Ian couldn't remember the last time he'd been so happy to see someone.

"Emma make bacon n' eggs," she beamed.

"For that I am very thankful," replied Ian sitting down in his usual spot. He surprised himself, with his feelings as well as the comments that accompanied them. He noted that the fire was glowing, the living room cleaned up and the place generally tidy.

"Emma, who cleaned up?" Ian was genuinely impressed. After all, he knew he wasn't the only exhausted one.

"Doc and Emma. Ian go to bed after pull Mr. Mac's leg. Doc and Emma clean up, then Doc go bed. Emma fix fire, clean up and take nap." She dropped some bacon onto another clean plate and set it before Ian.

He ate ravenously. Deliberately leaving food for Emma and Doc, Ian cut himself off before he was full. Whatever they had in the fridge would have to last until the roads were cleared. By the looks of things beyond his windows, it wouldn't be any time soon. He piled some more of each on his plate, walked over to the dogs and fed them each a slice of bacon and a pile of eggs.

"Emma, I never would have made it if it weren't for these beasts. They saved our lives last night."

Emma waited until she was done chewing to respond. "Pax and Rex good dogs. They help Emma." She smiled at them.

Ian straightened, set his dishes in the sink and donned his coat.

"I'm going to get some more wood."

"Be back in five?" asked Emma. Ian stood staring at her, letting out a guffaw when she gave him a knowing smile.

With the fire stoked and wood stacked, Ian checked on the patients. MacLean was resting peacefully with his right leg sticking off the couch at an angle. What they'd rigged up for a splint were the rake handle, garden tool and firehawk each wrapped in bath towels. They were positioned on the bottom portion of his leg equidistant from each other. His leg was then wrapped in towels and linen tablecloth until the tools could no longer be seen. The duct tape was wrapped around all of the above, tightly enough that MacLean would not be able to bend his knee and the tools wouldn't be able to move. Maybe he should get into medicine after all, that or package engineering.

The Doc said infection had begun setting in, so she bathed everything in brandy. The empty bottle was in the recycle bin to prove it. Beyond that, he remembered nothing more of the morning hours until he'd awakened on the hearth in his sleeping bag.

Ian pulled the tarp out from underneath the couch. Carrying it outside, he folded it in the muffled silence of the winter wonderland. After folding and putting away the tarp, he surveyed the valley beneath, taken aback by the immense quantity of snow that had fallen. Apparently there'd be more if he was accurately reading the heavy grey clouds above him.

Rubbing his hands as he went back into the house, he was struck by the rightness of its fullness. Only two people had ever been in Uplands other than his subcontractors. He had intended to invite Kat's family up when they'd gotten settled, but, well, he had been missing a wife that entire duration.

Before then, he and Kat hadn't ever been there long enough for her parents to make the trek from Colorado. Her brother, "California Kyle" the "surfer photogradude," as Ian called him, simply hadn't been on Ian's radar screen. As for Ian's own family, they were all gone. So, the only faces these mirrors had ever seen were Kat's and his own.

Never mind the fact they were all there as patients or caretakers, he liked having these mountain people in his home. He liked sharing Uplands a lot more than he thought he would.

Putting a few things away before sitting down next to the fire, he sat close enough to MacLean to hear him breathe. Doc emerged from above wearing Kat's clothes. A fresh pang of grief struck him.

"Do I smell bacon and eggs?" she asked Ian.

"You sure do, courtesy of Emma Waltham. She's quite the chef."

Doc finished the stairs and negotiated the dogs. As she turned the corner to the kitchen, the smells hit her full force. Ian got up to join her and make them all coffee. Emma knew her way around the Bausch, but not the French press.

"Emma," gasped Doc as she took a seat at the nook next to her, "this looks and smells delicious. Thank you!"

"Emma cook bacon n' eggs," she beamed.

"Well, I for one, am very thankful!" affirmed Doc. Ian grabbed a clean plate and fork, setting them before Doc.

Making coffee occupied him as he listened to the women. Not much of that had gone on in his life. He was an only child who had lost his parents while he was in college. His parents had both been rather reclusive. That was the price of being bright and quirky, you gave up on people. Ian ventured to guess that even his presence had been a mistake, but they'd taken that one on the chin and kept him. The numbers he was experiencing right now in Uplands was a new thing for him. It was the most people he'd ever had in any of his homes at one time.

"You were a real trooper last night, Emma. I don't know what we would have done without you. I was so tired I couldn't see straight. After Ian went to bed you helped me clean up and give the girls their shots. Now you're up getting everyone breakfast! You're amazing, Emma." She smiled at Emma as she filled her mouth with eggs.

"Emma help. Mr. Mac, Ruby, Pearl are friends." She got up and set her leftovers on the floor for her dogs. Ian didn't say a word.

Thankfully, Ian had visited the grocery store two days before the outage, so his refrigerator was well stocked. Even so, dog food hadn't been on the list. Pouring half-and-half into a creamer and setting out the sugar bowl, Ian handed Doc a mug and set another on the table for Emma and one for himself.

"Coffee, Emma?" he asked as he poured.

"No, thanks."

Having set the carafe back in place, he filled a glass with

water and handed it to Emma. Doc stirred in cream and sugar and pushed them over to Ian.

They all sat in the nook silently sipping.

Evening found Ian at the sink washing the supper dishes via lantern while Doc administered shots to the patients upstairs. A moaning brought Ian to MacLean's couch. He stepped into MacLean's line of vision just as the patient opened his eyes.

"Hey partner, how you feelin'?" inquired Ian.

"Like hell. What did you do, throw another tree at me?" He used his hands to maneuver his leg back on to the couch, then slid himself upright. Taking in his surroundings, Ian answered his unasked question.

"You're at my place. The roads are blocked, so I couldn't get you any further. As for your medical condition, the bone has been set and you're on antibiotics. Infection had begun, so this will be touch and go. The doctor is here, so you can get the gory details from her. All I know is, you got the best fireplace tool known to mankind attached to your leg, so you'd best heal quick." Ian talked as he made his way to the kitchen.

"Power is still out, so light comes at a premium around here." He came back to MacLean's side and handed him a glass of water. He downed it in one swallow, then winced.

"You got anything stronger than that?"

"I did, but your leg drank it." Ian sat down as Doc made her way down the stairs. She came around the couch and introduced herself to MacLean.

"Mr. MacLean, I'm Laura Tate." She stretched her hand toward him and smiled.

"Dr. Preston, for short," interrupted Ian from the kitchen.

"Glad to meet you, ma'am." He took her hand in his. "I guess I've got you to thank for attaching this picnic table to my leg."

Doc laughed and sat on the coffee table facing him. "Well,

Mr. MacLean, you had quite a fight with that tree. If you look this bad, I'd hate to see what the tree looks like." She leaned back and crossed her legs. "I don't know what Mr. Campbell was able to tell you, but you're not out of the woods yet. Pun intended. I reset the leg, but it still needs to be x-rayed. I didn't see any bone fragments, but there may be some, in which case you'd need some follow-up surgery. You probably will anyway, since you had a compound fracture. The bone was exposed to the air, as you may know. That's never a good thing, and you're no exception. Infection had begun setting in. I got your leg good and drunk with some vintage anti-bacterial and it's been doing some shots of penicillin, so the prognosis is good. If it weren't for Emma taking good care of you, and Mr. Campbell introducing the two of us, we'd be taking your measurements right now."

"So, am I gonna lose my leg, Doc?" MacLean was a man of black and white, no gray.

"Not if I can help it, Mr. MacLean. There's a good chance if we can get you to a hospital in the next twenty-four hours, that you'll be skipping the Light Fantastic this time next year."

MacLean leaned forward and squinted at her. "And what's the prognosis of that? Last I heard, we were snowed in under four feet of white wet."

Doc looked at Ian. Ian took over.

"Mr. MacLean, I think I have a plan. If the power doesn't come back on and or the road doesn't get plowed in the next twelve hours, I'm going to siphon the gas from my car and get you to the hospital via snowmobile. You may not remember it, but I used one to get you most of the way here. I ran out of gas in the woods about a half mile from here. I think I can transport you on the pallet with some rigged up skis. The biggest hitch to all this is that I don't know where the closest hospital is, nor how to get to it without roads. Hopefully, Doc here can help out with that part."

While Ian was revealing his plans to MacLean, Doc was heating some supper for them. They had an ample supply of broth, thanks to Ian's penchant for soup. She heated some from an open box, while dicing some vegetables to sauté in the saucepan. Before long, translucent onions and celery, along with some greens, made it into the broth. She made enough for six, in case she had more patients waken during the night. After this long sleep, they would be famished. She handed a bowl and spoon to Ian who gave her a quizzical look, then filled him in on her concerns.

"Listen, I think I'm going to waken the patients in the morning. Right now their hydration levels are adequate, but if I don't get liquids in them soon, they won't be. I brought lots of supplies, but not enough IVs to see us through this many people being IV dependent this long. Just thought I'd let you know what my intentions are." After filling some bowls with broth, she placed them on a tray with spoons and straws.

Ian took in her tired form.

"Sure, Doc, whatever you think best." He put down his bowl.

"Let me give you a hand." He picked up a lantern from the kitchen and lighted the way.

"Emma," Doc softly spoke as they entered the room, "Mr. MacLean is awake. Would you like to see him? I'll sit here with Pearl and Ruby."

Emma immediately got up and made her way down the stairs. Ian watched as Doc gently pulled Pearl's hair away from her face. The kindness of such a gesture struck him. The child was not awake, nor would she ever know someone had done something so small. Yet, it was the very smallness of it, the unnecessary and unprescribed nature of it, that made the kindness so large. Kat had done that sort of thing, not just to a sleeping form, but to a dying one. Not just to one, but many. What ilk of goodness did it require to pour oneself into others day after day, not only to go unnoticed, but perhaps unthanked – because your patient did not live.

A slight rustle from the bed brought Ian's attention back to his own patients. What was a grimace yesterday, he noticed, had become a peaceful visage today. The fever was still present, but no longer had the upper hand. Doc took their temperatures again and checked their blood pressure for what he hoped was the last time.

"Are my eyes deceiving me, or are they looking better, Doc?" Although the scarlet tinge of sickness was ebbing, Ian was not sure the girls were free from danger.

"Truthfully," Doc began as she carefully tucked sheets and blankets around the sleeping forms, "another day behind us would give me an easier night sleep." She straightened up and stretched her back. "MacLean, though, now he's another story. I've seen worse, but not much. Whether the infection responds to penicillin shots and vintage port remains to be seen. His prior state of health, which seems to be excellent, and his Scottish temperament, which seems tenacious, will be of tremendous account. It could make the difference."

Ian grabbed another quilt out of the closet. "The difference between a leg or prosthesis?"

She stared at him over the sleeping forms. "No, Ian, between life and death."

Chapter 20

EXTREME MAKEOVER

Other than MacLean's cold sweats and painful grunts, the house was warm and quiet. With the patient only feet away, Ian could see and hear his struggle. His body fought the fever with clenched fists, while his mind attempted to placate the pain. There was no remedy at hand. Everything Doc could do had been done. The rest was up to MacLean's grit and Ian's resourcefulness. Getting MacLean to a hospital seemed to be the only missing piece to his recovery. When Ian had mentioned his plans to get MacLean to a hospital, Doc had questioned the efficacy of moving him again.

"Ian, I think moving him again at this juncture would do more harm than good," Doc patiently offered. Ian couldn't believe what he was hearing. Peppering her with cross-examination questions came naturally under the circumstances.

"Aren't there more potent antibiotics to be offered? Couldn't they put him on massive, intravenous doses? Wouldn't that make his prognosis a great deal better at this point?"

"Yes, yes, and yes, but we're not talking about being medevacced out, Ian. We're talking about you jerry-rigging an antique snowmobile that you think ran out of gas, five miles to a destination you've never been, across terrain you don't know.

159

That kind of trip would entail stressful movement and possible re-injury. All of Hamish's energy and cellular activity would be refocused to keep him warm and stable that would otherwise have been used to heal." She looked closely at Ian to determine if he was listening or just giving her ear service.

"It's not an either or proposition, Ian. Holistically, there are a lot of other factors to consider, not the least of which, is getting lost or breaking down out in that winter wasteland and *both* of you winding up dead."

Ian wasn't used to losing arguments, but he had the stinging sensation he just had. Doc's reasoning had seemed sound. Perhaps he was still laboring under stress and lack of sleep and wasn't thinking clearly.

"I'll sleep on it."

That was precisely what Ian wanted to do, he just didn't know where to do it. With Emma using his bed, Doc taking up residence in the study, Ruby and Pearl in the guest bed, and MacLean on the downstairs couch, there was no room left in the inn. To the sounds of Doc toiling in the kitchen, Ian returned to his bedroll before his fireplace surrounded by the dogs, and slept through breakfast.

By late afternoon, all three caretakers had reawakened from their midday slumbers. Emma was seated on a nearby chair staring at Ian.

"What for lunch, Ian?"

It was the first time Ian could remember Emma asking for help in any way, shape or form. Ian considered that Emma was a woman of routine. Breakfast was her thing at Uplands, but any other meal, any other time of day, and she was out of her element. He could hear the shower running and assumed Doc was getting her daily ablutions.

With his company ready for their next square and three still out of commission, Ian considered what to piece together for a meal, and how to fix the massive problems before them.

Twenty minutes later, soups and salads devoured, Ian found himself, once again, in the kitchen with Emma. By lamplight, they were washing and drying the dishes and putting them away when Doc came down to join them. Finding the kitchen cleaned, Doc turned on the gas under the teapot and took a seat in the nook beside Emma.

"I noticed you don't have a television. Other than read all those books you've got under lock and key, what do you do for entertainment around here?" Doc asked.

Ian carefully folded the dishtowel over the range handle. "Lots of things that a Molly Pitcher like you would find utterly boring," Ian responded. While Emma sipped in silence, Doc continued her query.

"Okay, how about work. What kind of law do you practice?"

He turned to face her, leaning against the Smeg. "I'm retired now. I used to practice criminal defense law primarily. Occasionally, my clients needed help with other matters, which I might or might not handle for them. But the bulk of my practice was criminal defense." Ian adjusted the lantern wick to provide more light in the darkening kitchen.

"You don't seem the type. I was thinking contracts, patents, insurance ... you know *Paperchase*. What drew you to criminal defense?"

"A knack. I interned at the Massachusetts Supreme Court one summer and determined very quickly that I preferred the courtroom to the computer screen. To make sure, I did my next internship with a large litigation firm and specifically asked to be assigned the attorney who logged the most courtroom hours." Ian filled a bowl with water and placed it on a mat on the floor next to the refrigerator. Doc smiled to herself wondering when Ian had finally given in to the inevitability of the dogs. He continued.

"I assisted him on two cases that summer, one of which lasted a month. I loved it. I loved the strategy, the action, the thinking on your feet, the jury angle, the personality dynamics, the whole thing. From there, it evolved to working with difficult people in powerful positions with lots of money behind them. The firm needed someone with the trial skills and the people skills to deal with the mafia and the primadonnas. I excelled at it and capitalized on it once I'd won a few cases for some big names. After that, it was simply the snowball effect."

"Were your parents lawyers?"

"Ha, are you kidding? No. They probably rolled over in their graves when I tried my first criminal defense case."

"Then why law in the first place?"

"I made the mistake of asking my Dad what I was good at doing, what he thought my employable skills were."

"And?"

"And after thinking long and hard, he said, 'reading.'"

"What else?"

"That was it: reading."

Doc stopped sipping the tea she'd been holding. Ian could see her considering and saw a smile emerge. She poured more steaming water into her teacup and carried on.

"So if you were such a good reader how come you didn't go into editing or journalism or something?"

Ian wiped down the counters, put the last of the dishes away, and leaned against the sink as he answered Doc's questions.

"That thought occurred to me, but just as quickly I dismissed it. I wanted to shape and control *my* future with my career choice. I didn't want to report on *other* people's mishaps or adventures, read about *other* people's hard work and print it. I didn't want to spend all my waking hours helping other people advance *their* lives, control *their* destinies."

"You mean, unlike criminal defense where you keep *other* people from losing jobs, going to jail, or ending up on death row? Where *other* people's liberty and lives are on the line?"

Ian noted the sarcasm. "I see your point, Doc, but I made enough money assisting those *other* people with their lives, 'controlling them,' if you will, that I was able to shape and control my own."

"These clothes are beautiful, Ian!" Kat marveled at the contents of her walk-in closet. Drawers, cabinets, hangers, all displayed new and lovely designs and textures: Extreme Makeover, Closet Edition.

Ian was proud of himself. He'd spent hours considering Kat's coloring: hair, eyes, skin, to find the perfect complementary shades. He'd researched the shapes and sizes charts: tall, thin, with just the right amount of curves, in order to determine the best styles for her shape. He'd even consulted the fashion coordinator at Sak's, Brooks Brothers', and Macy's to ensure that the remaking of Kat Campbell was a blockbuster. He beamed.

"Thanks. Just a few things I threw together that I thought would look nice on you. He snapped his fingers and picked up a small album at his elbow. "And one of the best features of the whole thing is this!"

Kat had seated herself on one of the vanity stools admiring the handbags behind the lighted cabinetry. Ian placed the book in her lap and leaned over her, turning pages as he spoke.

"These are pre-coordinated outfits arranged by time of day and event. Let's say you're invited to a luncheon at the Courtyard. You would flip to this divider entitled, "Day Fine Dining," and turn the separated pages for a piece by piece look at the different combinations of skirts and blouses. It's perfect! No more thinking involved, and haphazardly choosing what looks most inviting for the occasion."

Kat's face had lost all traces of excitement. Her eyes searched the room then settled on Ian as she turned to face him. "So, just like the child's "exquisite corpse" books, you've pre-arranged and coordinated my outfits, so I don't have to think about what to wear?"

"Yeah," Ian beamed, "isn't it great?"

"Where are my clothes, Ian?" Kat stood up, indicating the tour was over.

"What do you mean? They're right here, Kat, from floor to ceiling." He turned to take in the shoes, handbags, sweaters, gowns; the full assemblage of his wife's new look.

"No, Ian, these are clothes you bought for me. I'll repeat the question, counselor. Where are my clothes?"

"Oh, those," Ian waved dismissively, "I asked the doorman to take them to Goodwill."

BETSY BOYD LESLIE

Chapter 21

GOODWILL

Yet again, Ian awoke to blinking lights, only these weren't red taillights or white headlights, they were yellow plow lights. He jumped out of the sleeping bag next to the hearth, tripped over Rex, and looked out the living room window. The black ribbon running up the white mountain gave him a thrill.

After checking the kitchen clock for a 6:30 a.m. time, he fed the fire and rolled up his bag. MacLean had been in such pain throughout the night, that Ian had slept nearby to ensure he didn't do anything crazy. He'd had to help him to the bathroom a couple times, too, which the women weren't qualified to do.

His wasn't the only company MacLean had. Both dogs curled up next to Ian and his bag until it was hard to tell whether Ian was covered in bag or dog.

He put the water on and beat Emma to the breakfast punch. There were limited eggs and bacon left, so he improvised with cheese omelets and toast. The French press was pressed into service for coffee for four or more.

Before long, the scents wafting upstairs did their work and the kitchen was filling with clients.

"Emma make breakfast, Ian." Emma looked hurt.

"Look, you've been working so hard I thought I'd treat you for a change. Have a seat and let me serve you, Emma."

"Here, here," echoed Doc. "It's about time Ian pulled his weight around here, Emma. You just sit back and relax for a change." She helped herself to some coffee and set the sugar out for community use. Emma sat in her usual spot and began spooning some omelet onto her plate.

"Well, nurse Waltham and nurse Campbell, I'm going to need …" began Doc.

"Whoa, whoa, Doc, before you start recruiting again, I gotta tell ya, I got a new gig working with the Yellow Cab Company."

"What?" Doc stopped sipping her coffee and looked at Ian for explanation.

"Ladies, take a look out the front window and tell me what you see." They both made their way to the window and looked out. Emma looked confused, so Doc immediately pointed it out for her.

"Emma, look, the road is plowed!" She pointed to the ribbon of asphalt making its way to Uplands.

Ian had followed them over and was gazing out over their shoulders. "After we eat, I'll start shoveling my drive. It'll take a while, but we'll get 'er done. By lunch time I'm hoping to have anyone in the hospital who needs to be and you home, Doc."

They all walked back to the breakfast nook and finished their repast.

"Ian, I'm not sure the girls need moving. There's nothing more that can be done for them in a hospital other than hydration, which Emma and I can do for them here. Besides, they probably don't have insurance to pay for the care. They'll be better off here by all accounts. Would that be a problem?"

Ian gave it some thought. "You tell me what needs to be done, and if Emma will stay, I think the two of us can handle it."

"You don't understand. I don't need to leave. I had the week off this week anyway and don't need to be anywhere. I'll just grab some things from town when you take MacLean, and come back here with you after we've got him checked in."

Ian pushed his plate away and considered her offer. "What kind of recuperation are we talking about?"

"As of this morning, both are fever free. I'm going to wake them up when I go upstairs if they aren't awake already. Emma and I will feed them some soup and get them hydrated throughout the day. If we stay on that course, I can see them up and around in three or four days, possibly able to return home with some care and supervision by the beginning of next week."

"Let me get this straight. You and Emma would both stay here for the next week caring for Ruby and Pearl, after which, they should be able to return home with a little help there, too, presumably Emma." Doc was nodding her head.

"Emma help." Of course, thought Ian, could you do anything but?

"Let me think on it while I shovel. In the meantime, Emma, you need to get a nice, hot bath. I set some clothes out for you last night that you may not have noticed." Before he'd retired to the living room floor, he'd changed the sheets on his own bed and gotten the bedroom and bath ready for Emma. He mentioned the clothes, but she didn't take the hint. Clearly, he was going to have to take a more direct approach. "Use my bathroom and dress in the clothes on the stool. They'll be a little long, but they should work."

Emma was a little wider around than the other women, so Ian had looked through his own collection of sweats to lend her. He couldn't wait for the power to come back on so he could get some washing done. Before the week was out, they'd start looking like a pajama convention.

While Doc and Emma bore a tray of liquids upstairs, Ian headed outside. He strapped on the snowshoes to get to the storage shed for his shovel. Beginning behind his Range Rover, he shoveled for the next two hours, winding his way down the driveway to meet the mountain pass. It was tortuous work. His muscles still ached from his day- long rescue and the marathon chopping event the day before. About the time he thought he needed a break, Emma came to him with a steaming mug.

"Found hot chocolate, Ian." She grinned as she handed him the mug. The warmth seeped through his gloved hands, reminding him how cold he was.

"Thanks, Emma. How are Ruby and Pearl? Did they wake up and eat?"

"Yes. Ruby and Pearl ate all the soup Doc made. Ruby got to the bathroom, but Pearl back to sleep."

"Great! I'm glad to hear it, Emma." He took another long sip, hoping to give the mug back to Emma to take back inside. "Emma, was it scary taking care of them? All three of them were counting on you, Emma."

"Emma not scared. Pray God send help. God did. Send Ian." She grinned, took his cup and walked away. She left a fresh almond scent behind, the scent of the soap in Ian's bath. With the scent lingering, he checked to see what she was wearing. Either she or Doc or both had kept Ian's sweatpants from dragging through the snow by duct taping the excess at the ankle. He had to chuckle at the sight. Kat would never believe it. For that matter, Kat wouldn't believe any of this. He resumed shoveling to work off the thought.

Another hour later, Ian returned the shovel to the storage shed. He grabbed the keys from the mudroom and started up the car. While it warmed up, Ian scrubbed snow and ice from the windows and put the seat heaters into action. That was one feature that had sold him on the model. The back seat was lowered so that MacLean could simply lay down in the back. Sitting simply wouldn't be an option. He switched off the engine, pocketed the keys and made tracks for lunch.

"I figured you'd be famished after digging your way through Antarctica." Doc pushed a grilled cheese sandwich at him as he spooned some more Tomato and Basil Soup into his mouth.

"Your patients were cooperative this morning, I heard. Where are they now?" Ian was gobbling his food in an effort to get MacLean to the hospital without further ado.

"They were all up at one point and Emma and I were feeding and watering as fast as possible. Ruby got up and visited with MacLean while he ate. They were all so exhausted from the effort that they're all napping again."

"I'm glad to hear it, Doc. When I saw that kid two days ago I wasn't sure if she was coming or going."

"Speaking of which, I'm glad you're going into town. MacLean's leg is red and warm to the touch. I'm afraid your brandy wasn't old enough." Arms akimbo and eyebrows knitted, Ian could tell Doc was worried.

"Then let's get this show on the road. Are you sure the ladies are well enough to stay here?"

"I'm sure of it."

"And you're okay with Emma acting as head nurse?"

"After watching her with these people, I'm convinced she'd do a better job than I."

Ian cogitated. This was all new territory for him. Saving people, hosting people, mending people, and all in his dear Uplands. Now he was being asked to leave it in their hands while he spent his Christmas Eve carting a Scottish curmudgeon to town.

"Well then," he took one last sip and stood up, "what are you waiting for, Doc? Get your boots on."

As Doc hopped up to get prepared for the outing, Ian made his way over to MacLean. Wide eyed and grimacing, MacLean addressed Ian.

"I heard it all. Let's get movin'."

He attempted to stand and Ian had to steady him as he careened to the side. They hobbled to the mudroom where Ian dressed MacLean in some of his ski garb. By the time Ian and MacLean were both dressed, Doc had joined them at the door.

"Got a free hand, Doc?" Ian asked from under MacLean's arm.

"Yep, whatcha need?"

"Grab that sleeping bag I put in the first cupboard under the mudroom mirror."

"Will do."

Ian virtually had to carry MacLean down the two steps and over to the car. He opened the back hatch, turned MacLean to sit in the car facing outward and then got in the car himself to pull MacLean in from the front. Between the two of them, MacLean was in with only two yells. Doc opened the sleeping bag and laid it out over MacLean's form.

Ian and Doc hopped in the front and threw their gear at Doc's feet. Neither were going anywhere without their emergency kits. Not after these two days.

Carefully and slowly, as to jerk MacLean's body around as little as possible, Ian wove his way down the mountain. Doc gave him directions to a hospital two towns away. Although it wasn't the closest, it was the best at what MacLean needed. He'd get better care at the further one.

Ian pulled into the emergency lane and parked with his hazards on. Doc hopped out and within minutes had two orderlies with a gurney extricating MacLean. Ian drove around to the parking lot and found a spot that he could drive straight through if it started to snow again. He didn't want to be kept from going back to his Uplands ... and Emma.

When he found his way to the welcome desk, they pointed to the disappearing forms of Doc and MacLean's gurney. He jogged down the hall to catch up.

"They did a rush admittance when they saw his leg and I told them who I was. They're taking him straight to x-ray. He'll be in surgery within the hour if it's needed." It struck Ian that Doc still looked tired. Even though her patients were sleeping, she'd still been getting up every four to six hours to administer antibiotics and check vitals. She hadn't had a decent night sleep in four days. Ian felt that now familiar pang of regret.

"I think I'll stay here, Ian, until they've figured out what they're going to do and do it. If I need a ride, I can call a cab or get someone here to drive me home. It may be a while."

Ian was astonished. "Are you kidding? You just spent the last two, or is it three days, nursing these complete strangers, you're exhausted, you finally get to hand one of them off to someone more qualified than yourself to care for them and you're going to stick around?" He couldn't believe what he was hearing.

"Ian, he's not a stranger anymore. Besides, he has no next of kin. Emma and the girls are his only friends, his only family. If I leave, he'll have no one advocating for him or smiling at him when he wakes up. You and Emma will do just fine taking care of the girls. They're gems as patients."

Ian sat down in the chair closest to him. He was so used to the dim natural lighting of the house, that the anesthetic white walls and fluorescent lights were giving him a headache.

"Do you have your phone?" When he realized how ridiculous his train of thought was in light of the power outage, he back-pedaled. "Okay, strike that. What time is it now?"

She looked down at her watch. "Almost two."

"I'll stay for one hour. At the end of that hour I am leaving whether we have news or not. I'm going to the grocery store and buy supplies, go home and make supper and come back here and get you at six o'clock. Do you savvy?" His face was resolute.

"Ian, I'll be fine. I'll just grab a cab ..."

"I didn't ask if you'd be fine," he interrupted, "I asked if you savvied."

"No, I don't savvy. I'll find my own way to my own home, change and drive up."

"What year and model car do you have?" When Doc stalled, Ian reiterated.

"You heard me, what year and model car do you have?"

"1987 Mazda 2 door sedan light blue with a dark blue vinyl interior. Why?"

"That settles it. We're following my plan, not yours." He leaned back in his chair, reached for a magazine and began thumbing through the recipe pages.

"You are exasperating!"

"So I've heard. I wasn't paid to be a patsy. Now sit down and help me figure out what the girls, as you call them, would like for Christmas dinner."

Ian slammed the door. "What the hell is that winter rat doing in your parking space, Kat? I thought we agreed that you were not loaning your space anymore." He tossed his keys on the counter and slammed his briefcase into a waiting chair. "A portion of the astronomical fees I pay on this place are for covered parking next to the elevators. That means your car, and my Mercedes, not my Mercedes and some 70s throwback with doors the size of Texas that knick mine when they're opened! They're for us, Kat, not charity."

Kat turned from her meal preparations. She considered his heavy breathing, his scowl, his clenched fists.

"So let me make sure I heard you correctly. Did you say, 'your' parking space."

"Yes."

"As in Kat Campbell's?"

"Well, of course. By way of monthly payments."

"Whatever they're 'by way of,' you've agreed it's my parking space, right?"

"Right, but not for you to go giving it away."

"Alfred cannot safely walk from the parking garage to our building. It's got four different sets of stairs and three different path elevations between here and there. It was already a challenge before his knee replacement surgery and now it's downright dangerous. He slipped and fell two weeks ago."

"Kat, you can appeal to the board and get him a new spot."

"I did. That is his new spot." Kat took a moment to rummage through the fridge and find a zucchini. She closed the door and looked at him. "Just look at it this way, Ian. I donated the parking space to Goodwill."

Chapter 22

CHRISTMAS EVE

"Doctor Tate?" inquired a young intern with a mask settled around his neck.

Doc awoke and sat up. "Yes? How is he?"

"The surgery is over and Mr. MacLean is in recuperation. You can join him there in a minute. You did a fine job setting the break, all things considered." Doc wasn't sure whether to take that as a slap on the back or a slap in the face.

"Given the location and severity of the break, I had to put some rods and screws in place. There was infection beginning, but I think you got a handle on it just in time. We'll see over the next couple days. That little marinade trick you pulled may have saved his leg, maybe even his life. Congratulations."

As he stepped away, she let her face fall into her hands and she wept. When she awoke, she had no idea how long she'd been asleep. She came to with a jolt, grabbed her belongings, and rushed to Recovery. Her accidental timing was perfect; MacLean was just coming to.

He opened his eyes and looked into hers. "Am I alive?"

Her grin spread from cheek to cheek. "Very much so, Mr. MacLean."

"Damn," he slurred his way through the rest of his

173

comments, "I always heard if you saw bright lights and purdy girls you'd made it to heaven."

"That may be, but I ain't purdy and you're not dead."

She settled into the chair next to his bed and waited. It would be another thirty minutes or more before his anesthesia wore off. She wanted to be right there to see him through the after effects.

MacLean fell back to sleep and so did Doc. Head on Mac's bed, the nurse had to take his blood pressure on the awkward side of the bed to keep from disturbing her. By six o'clock, both were alert and carrying on a conversation. She was intrigued by his stories and entertained by his humor. Ian walked in on them laughing.

"Well, I guess you pulled through," Ian jabbed at MacLean.

"Yeah, it was touch and go, but my acidic personality saw me through. Hey, I understand your marinade saved my life. What brand and year was it exactly?" Ian told him.

"Did it have a gold label with a bagpipes emblem?" MacLean pressed.

"I think so, but I couldn't say for sure. I've still got the bottle. Would you like me to save it for you?"

"I sure would. It has some sentimental value to me." He had a faraway look in his eye that Ian attributed to home health surgeries.

"Well, Doc, your cab is here. You ready to vamoose?"

"Yep." She stood with her coat in her hands and addressed MacLean. "Someone will be back to check on you tomorrow, okay?"

"Sounds good, Doc. I ain't one for places like this. I gotta get outa here pronto. Put in a good word for me, would ya?"

Doc smiled at him, "Hamish, you need to be here for a while. It's important that you rest and let the doctors and nurses do what their trained to do."

"I can't promise that, Doc," replied MacLean, "These places give me the creeps. I'm mighty grateful, for all you done for me."

Ian wouldn't swear to it in a court of law, but he thought he saw some moisture develop in the corner of Mac's eye. Ian put his hand in his pocket to find his keys, when he was reminded of the contents.

"I almost forgot!" He pulled out a miniature snow globe, wound the key at the bottom, shook it a tad and placed it on the table next to MacLean. The strains of White Christmas filled the room. It took MacLean a moment to gather himself.

"Tomorrow's big doin's. You all stay put. I'll be fine." MacLean brushed his eye nonchalantly.

"Right then. I'm glad we understand one another. We'll be back tomorrow." And she leaned down and kissed his cheek.

They slammed the doors shut and buckled up.

"I thought of a compromise, Ian. Obviously, the blue interior isn't what worries you, but the fact that the age of a car doesn't work the same way as it does with brandy. You're worried my car can't handle these conditions or worse ones if it snows again."

"You got me there, Doc." He leaned forward and started the car to get the heater going.

"So, you take me home, wait for me to gather some things and *follow* me up to your place. That way if the roads stay passable you don't have to do all the driving, especially if it's one way." She smiled at him, hoping for an affirmative response.

"I'll go for that. Now where do we go from here, Garmon?"

Ian couldn't believe the smoke coming out of the backside of the Mazda. Surely it wouldn't pass state inspection. How did it this year? Thankfully, they only had one more turn to make before they were back at Uplands. He couldn't wait to see the look on Doc's face when she walked in the door.

"Ian, it's beautiful! How did you do all this in so short a

time?" Doc walked around the eight foot tree admiring the lights. She'd never seen a tree this big out side a forest or hotel. It was stunning in breadth and beauty. It seemed as though there were hundreds of lights on it. Nestled in the far corner of the room from the front door, the lights twinkled and reflected off the window on the left side of the fireplace. It was beautiful to behold.

"Some elves helped me." He was beaming, too.

"How did you get it to light? The power's still off, right?"

"I bought a huge rechargeable battery pack for outages. I figured I'd need it again some day, so I made the investment."

She continued to gape at the tree. While at the hospital she had considered going home and sleeping in her own place for the night. She'd decided against it, since she'd already agreed to stay here. Now she was glad she'd stuck to her word.

"Has Emma seen it?"

"Are you kidding? She was one of my elves!"

"Emma elf!" was heard from the top of the stairs. She came running down to admire the tree with Doc.

"Did you say, 'elves'?"

"Yep. You've never seen a kid string lights like our own Pearl Avery." He walked over to the couch and sat down admiring his own handiwork. The clock struck seven and he hopped off the couch.

"Ten minutes until supper everyone!"

Doc disappeared upstairs to check her charges. Emma followed suit.

Wielding a tray loaded with five steaming bowls, a round of wheat bread, spoons and napkins, Ian made his way up the stairs. The "girls" were up, Pearl in the bed and Ruby on a bench seat by the window, wrapped in a wool tartan lap blanket.

Doc had brought in chairs from the adjoining rooms until everyone had a seat. Bowls of chicken noodle soup were distributed with chunks of thick, warm, wheat bread. Doc bowed her head and began to pray. Emma followed suit and the other three bowed out of politeness.

"Heavenly Father, we thank You for this food and the

hands that prepared it. We thank You that Ruby and Pearl are healing so quickly. We thank You for the good news and good work done on Mr. MacLean today. Bless this food to our bodies and us to Your service. In Jesus's name, Amen."

At first one could only hear the clink of metal as spoons scooped up the healing broth. But as everyone asked questions about MacLean and bread was unceremoniously dipped in bowls, the conversation grew louder and the room grew warmer. Ian couldn't remember a better supper.

Throughout the evening, the mysteries of Waltham Peak were revealed, but only in part. Ruby, Pearl, and Emma each shared their chapters in the story.

"Pearl's my girl's girl," explained Ruby. "My girl, June, ran off and married some drunken deadbeat thinking that was her way off the mountain and into the big time. The only thing worthwhile he ever did for her was give her a Pearl." Ruby smiled faintly at her witticism. "When he saw he had a little one on the way, he left June to spend his income on his habits instead of his dependents. June was diagnosed with coronary heart disease shortly after Pearl was born. It was so severe, she couldn't work and care for Pearl with the sickness, so she moved back to Waltham's Peak to live with me. Between me and Mac and Emma Girl, we took care of June 'til the end, and little Pearl from the beginning."

"How did you come to live here to begin with, Ruby?" asked Doc.

"I worked for Ira Waltham when he passed," explained Ruby. "Back in the heyday, MacLean and I were two of twenty who worked on the premises. A number of them lived in the big house, so commuting to and from town wasn't an issue. Others only came up a day or two, so it wasn't an issue for them either. MacLean and I were the only two who worked here every day, who didn't live in the big house, so Mr. Waltham had our homes built along with a few others for employees like MacLean and me. There were several scattered between my place and Emma's, but the other homes either fell down or burnt down over the years. The others moved away after Waltham died, but us ... well, we had everything we needed right where we were."

Ian took in this cook-to-a-millionaire. Her wiry gray hair was now washed and pulled back in a soft bun at the nape of her neck. She wore Kat's sweats as few older women could. Ian estimated her age to be closer to seventy based on the history he'd just heard. But she was a buff seventy. Her shoulders and arms belied a life of lifting, chopping, pushing, and churning. Her hands weren't arthritic, rather, they were young, strong hands. She stood five feet seven, with an authoritative air. One got the impression Ruby could do whatever she set out to do. Her unflinching green eyes confirmed it. Ruby Grimm was hardy, German stock.

"MacLean was already here when I came on. He had this mountain looking like a paradise. Mr. Waltham needed a place to unwind, relax, find peace. MacLean made it for him. The Walthams could have charged admission to those gardens, they were that fantastic." She dipped her bread, took a bite and smiled proudly at the memory.

"No offense, Mr. Campbell, your place is beautiful," she paused and looked out the ten foot window to the expanse beyond as if she could see it, "but it's a mere shadow of what Waltham and MacLean built."

Ian was surprised he wasn't offended. He'd spent so much time, money and energy on Uplands, he'd like to think of it as more than a shadow. He remembered walking through the footprint of the Waltham home. Although he was looking at mere remnants, he could tell something remarkable had once stood there.

"Like I said," Ruby continued, "MacLean and I ran into each other pretty frequently, because I had my own kitchen garden and I was the cook. I tended the herbs and MacLean and I had to coordinate the vegetable garden and the fruit and nut tree seasons. He sowed, I reaped. It was a pretty good working relationship, really. We worked together to provide a bountiful and beautiful spread for the Walthams and their many guests."

She looked up to see if Ian and Doc were still engaged. Their nods assured her that they were, so she continued.

"You see, Waltham came here to get away, but he didn't leave business behind. He brought it with him. So many people came to visit during his 'vacations' that they would joke down at the train depot that he should have his own stop on the peak. Those were some good times. People bustling about, money easy to come by, people laughing and chatting in every corner. It was a good time." She smiled in a melancholy manner, reminiscing in her mind.

"You should have seen the day Emma was brought home." She looked over at Emma. She was expecting the grin that came with the telling of this story. Ian and Doc could tell this must have been a favorite of Emma's. Perhaps even frequently requested.

"Mrs. Waltham had already had four children during the earlier years of their marriage who were in their late teens and twenties. In the meantime, she'd had a miscarriage or two, which was devastating to her. When she carried Emma to term on the brink of forty, she was elated. The whole household was excited and prepared a feast. Mr. and Mrs. Waltham drove in with a train of cans dragging from their car and honking their horn to beat the band."

Emma stopped eating and listened in rapt attention.

"What Emma wearing, Ruby?" Emma grinned. Clearly, she knew the answer, but wanted to hear it again.

"Emma Girl, you were dressed in the fanciest white gown I ever saw. It was a baby ball gown with lace and pearls around your neck and wrists. You were the prettiest thing I ever saw."

"Tell us the rest, Nana!" pressed Pearl. Although she wasn't at full throttle, Pearl was alert and attentive. It was the most life Ian had ever seen in her. She too was familiar with the story, and knew it to be a good one.

"Well," Ruby had been merely informing up to this point, but now was warming to her subject, "they got out of the car at the fountain ... There used to be a circular drive with a fountain in the middle," Ruby added for clarification, "and walked aaalllll the way down the walk to the front door with fifty people in line to touch the baby as they went by. Staff, family, visitors, everyone. If you were there that day, you touched that baby and blessed it on the way into the house. I was at the very end of that line, cause I'd been in the kitchen when the announcement was made that they'd arrived. I chased all the other kitchen staff out before me, so I was the last one standing at the door when she came in the house."

"What did the baby do?" asked Emma and Pearl right on cue.

"You know what that baby did when she looked up at me? Ruby peered at Ian and Doc with a knowing wink.

"What did she do?" asked Ian and Doc simultaneously.

"That baby smiled at me." Ruby leaned back in emphasis. "Just two days old and that baby stuck a grin at me like I'd never seen."

"What you call Emma?" asked Emma.

"Because of that grin, I took to calling her "Grinna" for the first couple years. Ever since, she and I have been close as bread and butter, right Grinna?"

"Bread and butter, bacon and eggs," responded Emma. "Ruby Emma nurse, so now Emma is Ruby nurse."

"That's right," affirmed Ruby. "When she was a 'wee bairn,' as Mac would call her, if she got sick she didn't want anyone doting on her but me. I think I understood her better than most and she knew it. Or maybe it was them ginger snaps I always snuck to her. Little did I know she'd pay me back in spades. Me *and* my Pearl."

"Tell about garden," Emma insisted.

"Emma Girl, you're all done eating and I've barely started. You tell' em." With that, Ruby took a bite of bread.

In a faltering, but determined voice, Emma began. "Mister Mac let Emma help in garden."

Ian could picture that. No other young siblings around, no school for her special needs, no reading to pass the time, Emma would have found her way to the kitchen or the garden where she wouldn't be underfoot. Emma had found loving, attentive adults in those environments who had embraced her.

The cook and the gardener weren't her father's employees; they were her friends.

Ian wondered if that wasn't why Waltham ended up with a Disney World landscape, to give MacLean and his daughter something to do. Or perhaps he let MacLean have the lead in all things garden as a thank you for MacLean's love and care for Emma.

Either way, the Walthams loved their Emma, Ruby and MacLean loved their Emma, and the Walthams loved Ruby and MacLean for it. Ruby and MacLean had been too sincere in their kindness toward Emma to see the houses for what they were: gifts of gratitude.

"Emma help Mac build fountains, and plant rose gardens and orchards. It so pretty Emma sit in it. Emma swing and watch sunset," Emma finished.

"Where was your swing, Emma?" asked Pearl. She seemed familiar with these stories, as if they'd shared some of the history together in their cabins at night.

"Apple orchard other side." Emma pointed to the western wall of the house. Ian had seen that portion of the peak, but hadn't been as interested in it. Due to the previous Waltham estate having been at Uplands, it simply made for an easier construction. It had the better view, too just not of a sunset.

"Did you like to sit in your swing and watch the sunset?" confirmed Doc.

"Yep. Not winter. Too cold and windy." Emma emphasized her last statement with a "Brrr" and wrapped her arms around herself in mock shivering.

Ian could picture that. The wind had howled up that side of Waltham's Peak when he was there. Even on a calm day, it was windy on the west side. In the winter, it would have been brutal.

"Are any of these things still around?" asked Doc. "I mean, you said the grounds were extensive and included gardens, fountains and orchards. Do any of those things still exist?"

"Of course," offered Ruby, "most of what was left after the elements did their damage was bulldozed when this place went in, but there's still the apple orchard where Emma's swing was, some nut trees, a rose garden and the party gardens."

"All those are still here?" asked Ian.

"Not like they were in their day, but enough to identify them. We still use some of them," answered Ruby.

"I had no idea." Ian was surprised that he hadn't noticed or been told. Rogers was going to get another visit.

"Most people don't know," added Ruby. "When Mrs. Waltham died twenty years ago, Mr. Waltham got sick almost immediately and things started to decline. Nothing was the same after that. We know they were there because we remember them. No one else would notice."

Maybe Rogers wouldn't get that visit.

"I've got some pictures from the heyday I'll have to show you, Mr. Campbell. As a matter of fact, you can have them as a thank you gift. You could frame them as a part of Uplands' provenance."

Ian's mind was racing. Orchards, gardens, people - what a lively, lovely place Waltham's Peak must have been. He was glad to have heard this piece of Uplands history, and from someone who had lived it and loved it. Ruby, MacLean and Emma *were* the provenance.

Chapter 24

AMBULANCE CHASER

Ian cleaned the kitchen while Emma and Doc administered medicine and got everyone squared away with bedding. Ian felt funny sleeping on the couch after having just removed his patient that morning, so he opted for another night on the hearth with Pax and Rex. He was glad he'd taken the second trip to town to wash clothes.

Rather than run straight over to the grocery after dropping off Doc and MacLean, he'd come back up the mountain, collected all the dirty laundry, driven back and used six washers while he shopped. He'd never washed other people's clothes before. Going from zero to five took him a while.

That was one reason for the simple meal. It was a constructive dilemma: spend time on a fancy meal or spend time washing a small army's clothes. Considering the kind of laundry he had sitting in his hamper, there was no question which was more pressing. He knew he'd chosen well when all the ladies thanked him for their own clean clothes.

As he washed and dried in the light of the headlamp, the dogs snuffled through the kitchen looking for crumbs and slobbered over their water bowl. Ian tossed a paper towel over the new puddles and swept them up with his shoe.

He both dreaded and craved the morrow. Pearl would be well enough to come downstairs, Ruby would be well enough to feel like herself again, and Doc and Emma would be more rested and feel like themselves in their own clean clothes.

But Kat was nowhere to be found. She should be here with him at Uplands. She didn't belong anywhere else. She was his: his wife, his partner. How could she not feel the same way? Hadn't they finished law school together, weathered his partnership together, and built Uplands together?

He forced the questions and accusations from his mind. It had been a great Christmas Eve, such as it was. He didn't want to spoil it.

Ruby and Pearl had both gotten their first warm bath in days. They put on clean sweats, leaving their own laundered clothes for the following day. In their weakened condition, Emma helped them get dressed and tucked in, while Doc administered medicine and took vitals. They blew out candles and lamps as they shut the door behind them.

Emma departed toward Ian's room and Doc made her way downstairs.

"Watch out," Ian warned just in time, "the dogs' favorite spot is the bottom of those stairs. In the dark, they could be deadly speed bumps."

Doc pulled herself up short as she was descending the last stair, looked carefully and took a wide step in avoidance.

"As big as they are, you'd think you'd see them. Anything I can do to help?"

Ian dried his last bowl and put it away.

"Nope, I think I've got it licked."

She rolled her eyes and fell into a leather chair, "very punny. You know, this is really kind of you. I mean, you're probably used to entertaining and all, but not this kind of entertaining."

Ian pulled items out of the freezer and cupboards he would

need in the morning for his *pièce de résistance*. He didn't want to wake everyone in the morning as he prepared his Christmas culinary surprise.

"I don't entertain here. Uplands was meant to be a retirement home for my wife and me. We have only been in it a few times since its completion, so it hasn't really been broken in … until now. Entertaining wasn't even on the radar screen."

"Well, you do it like a pro. Used to it at home, I guess. After all, you were a partner in your firm. You would have needed to make a little rain. I assume entertaining was part of that process."

Ian stared at her dumbfounded. "What is it with you? Are you clairvoyant or something? I can see how you came up with that law thing to begin with, but 'partner'?"

"It's not remarkable at all, Ian. Just apply some good looking and listening skills and anyone can pull a Sherlock."

She ticked off her reasoning with all the fingers on her hand.

"You've got your study plastered with plaques and *pro bono* awards. The name of your firm includes yours. It isn't a stretch to assume the 'Campbell' is you, and if your name is on the stationary you must be a partner. How challenging is that logic? And how do partners become partners? By getting clients and winning cases. How do lawyers get clients if they don't chase ambulances? They schmooze. Where do lawyers schmooze? At parties their wives throw for them. So where did I depart from accuracy with that one?" She tucked her legs under her and waited for the correction.

"I seem to be driving ambulances now. What makes you think I didn't make my living chasing them?" He challenged.

"Your unfamiliarity with the hospital and medical terms. Your medical vocabulary would be as good as mine if it was part of your living. You couldn't even find your way to the bathroom at the hospital yesterday. No, you're no ambulance chaser."

"Touché." He set a large item in the sink and looked up. "Yes, I was a partner. No, my wife didn't throw parties. Yes, I

185

won cases. No, I didn't schmooze. The truth is, I don't like parties. I'm not much of a people person, so the last thing I wanted my wife to do was fill my house with them." He leaned against the refrigerator and finished his explanation.

"I worked for what was called a 'boutique firm.' I was good at winning, and was hired for that purpose. The firm had plenty of wealthy clients, they just didn't have a good win/loss ratio. That was where I came in. I won cases and turned that around for them. Ironically, I had the worst bedside manner, but ended up attracting the most clients. Why? Because word got out that our firm won. I won. No entertaining for me – just winning."

"So, if you were so good at it, how come you got out?"

Ian had gone back to rummaging. He was perusing the recipes and their ingredients to make sure he had what was called for. He turned and beamed Doc in the face with his lamp. He switched it off, carried the lantern over to the coffee table and sat down.

"If you must know, I got out because I won enough. I had a goal in mind when I wanted to retire and I met it. So, here I am to while away the rest of my life in lonely leisure. See how well I'm doing?" He had to smile in spite of himself.

"Uh-huh. I'm sure it's obvious to all objective observers. So, when will your wife be joining you?" She had hesitated with the last question, knowing full well it was none of her business.

A pause punctuated the question.

"I don't know." No one said anything for a moment. "I can't find her."

"You can't *find* her?"

"No, I can't." He murmured the response so faintly she almost didn't hear it.

"Do you mean 'find' as in she's lost, or 'find' as in kidnapped, or 'find' as in ran away, or what?"

Ian pulled the tattered letter out of his pocket. He had been carrying it with him every day. He wanted desperately to share it with someone. He wanted their support. He wanted their condolences. He wanted their help. On the other hand, he didn't want anyone to see his shame or pain. Really, it was embarrassing and he wasn't ready for it to come out in the light.

Doc finished reading the letter and carefully refolded it.

"If she's trying so hard to hide," she asked as she handed the letter back, "why are you trying so hard to find her?"

Ian considered before answering. "Initially, because she was my wife, my best friend. Frankly, the only person I cared to spend time with, could tolerate." Ian looked away for a moment. "Now I realize it's because she's the best thing that ever happened to me."

BETSY BOYD LESLIE

Chapter 25

CHRISTMAS PRESENCE

Ian rolled over to a wet lick. Rex needed to go out. No alarms, no bacon and eggs, it was Rex's dental treatment that got him off the floor. He had learned over the last three days that there was no denying the dogs. Once they decided it was time for relief, there was only one thing for it.

He rolled out of his sleeping bag, pushed the hair out of his face and made his way to the front door. To save time later, he softly whistled for Pax and let them both out. While Rex and Pax were relieving themselves, Ian gathered some wood for the fire and built it up.

He opened a door on the bottom of the china cabinet in the dining room and withdrew some boxes. They were beautifully wrapped boxes complete with festive paper and bows. It had brought him more joy than he'd expected just to think through what someone with little might want and hunt it down in the confines of the Birch village shopping district.

Gift buying for Kat was a cinch. She had a model's face and frame with gregarious green eyes and rich brown hair. She looked gorgeous in anything she wore. When they'd gotten married, he'd revamped her wardrobe, taking her from what he referred to as a "gypsy grunge" look, to something chic and alluring. He'd filled her closet with greens, browns, and golds. He knew her sizes in every style and frequently brought home the latest fashion for her. The closet upstairs was a testimony to his good taste and generous provision.

Thrusting thoughts of Kat from his mind, he gently placed the gifts under the tree, positioning them so they could be seen from the top of the stairs. This was one day he wasn't going to think of her or look for her, the one day it would hurt the most to be missing her. When the boxes were in place, he let in the dogs, fed them both breakfast and began preparing dinner.

Bird in oven and kitchen clean, he stepped aside as Emma entered the room.

"Emma make bacon 'n eggs."

"That sounds great, Emma. I'm famished." He had worked up an appetite working on the later meal. "I'll make coffee over here out of your way." A smile was forming as he thought about the four dozen eggs he'd purchased and the pounds of bacon he'd ordered from the deli.

"Emma, who gave you your dogs?" inquired Ian as he poured grounds in the press. The idea, along with numerous others, had been plaguing him.

"Daddy." Most of the time when Ian asked her a question, she stopped working to respond. This time was no exception. The burning eggs made Ian wish he'd let her work in silence.

He decided not to question her further until she had a free moment. It was the first morning he and Emma had had alone since before the storm. Somehow it felt like old times, but better. Now he wasn't wishing her away.

Hours later when Doc finally emerged from upstairs she had Ruby with her. From the landing, Ruby gasped at the beautiful tree. Doc grabbed her arm PT style and steadied her as they descended. The light from the window was sufficient to illuminate their path, but not enough to diminish the effect of the tree and its myriad lights.

"How'd you manage it, Mr. Campbell? It's beautiful," admired Ruby as she stood dwarfed by the tree.

"It wasn't easy. First, I made sure everyone slept for days

190

on end so they wouldn't discover my surprise as I arranged it. Then I stayed up real late last night to let the elves in, and cleared the fireplace for Santa's descent. Keeping Pax and Rex at bay was the hardest part, because they wanted a piece of Santa. It was a real challenge, Ruby, but I managed."

"Come on, Ruby, I'll sit you right here at the dining room table and bring you some food. That way you can enjoy the tree while you eat some of Emma's special breakfast."

Ian covered the mahogany table with placemats, while Emma filled plates. They gathered breakfast items to dine in the dining room, and Doc went back upstairs to return minutes later with Pearl.

When he heard the bedroom door shut, Ian raced to the bottom of the stairs. He wanted to see the look on Pearl's face when the tree hove into Pearl's view. Beckoning to Emma and Ruby, they too got up to enjoy the spectacle.

They saw Pearl before she saw them. Her small frame seemed so fragile. Although her color had improved, she was still a ghostly pale against the petal pink of Kat's sweats. She clung to Doc and reached for the railing. Her eye caught her grandmother at the foot of the stairs, then Emma, then Ian, then the tree.

"Oh, Nana! Isn't it beautiful!" She stood up straight and took in the tree with eyes wide and mouth agape.

"Merry Christmas, Pearl!" announced Ian.

"Merry Christhmas, Pearl!" shouted Emma

"Merry Christmas, Pearl Girl," said Ruby.

Aside from holidays with Kat's family, this was the most people Ian had ever had around his table. The silver clinking against china and easy, happy banter around the table was warming. It gave Ian a pleasure he hadn't remembered experiencing before. Not with clients, not with partners, not with family. This was new. He wasn't sure why or what he was feeling, he just knew he liked it.

He leaned back in his chair after his last bite of deli bacon and watched. There was an easiness to the women's interactions that he admired. He couldn't chalk all of it up to familiarity, because Doc had known them all of 72 hours, yet she fit right in. He couldn't chalk it up to ethnic, cultural, or social ties. These women ran the gamut of different backgrounds, hometowns, and intellects.

Curly Doc was laughing at memories of Emma and Pearl getting into trouble eating all of Ruby's carrot crop. Ruby chortled at Doc explaining her attempt to find a hospital in Africa in a city where no one spoke English. They all chimed in and listened in turn while Ian eavesdropped.

The light from the tree shone on Pearl's locks. Ian figured she was a pretty girl when she was well. She still was not herself, he decided. She had only eaten about ten bites of scrambled eggs. Wrapping her sweater about herself, she drew up her knees and huddled in her chair for warmth. Ian took that as a cue to refuel the fire.

"So, how about you, Ian. What funny or embarrassing story do you have?" Doc asked from the table.

The dogs' new favorite reclining area was the Christmas tree. He stepped over them now on his way back to the table.

"Me?" He honestly couldn't come up with anything. Stories of things gone wrong weren't funny to him, but irritating. What others may have seen as humorous were shortcomings to him, memories best left unremembered.

"None, really. I can't think of anything."

"Surely you've made mistakes or done something wrong or …" Ian cut Doc off in midsentence.

"Probably, yes, but I didn't find humor in those moments. Still don't." He began clearing the dishes.

"Probably?" Doc challenged. The ladies were dropping utensils on to plates and handing Ian their dishes.

"You know what I mean. Of course, I have, I just don't make a mental note of them to share with everyone later." Carrying the dishes into the kitchen, Ian carefully considered whether that was normal. Did everyone find mistakes funny?

Awkward moments laughable? Errors hilarious?

The women giggled and chatted freely as they finished clearing the table. This was a sight better, Ian thought, than the days they lay comatose in their bed.

"Ladies, our social calendar is packed today, so, please don't overstay your excursions inland," began Ian as he addressed the women relaxing on the couches. He was wearing a safety whistle and Raybans while clutching a clipboard in one hand and a pencil in the other.

"We have games and shows poolside this morning for your enjoyment," he gestured to the window and the snow piled against it. Pretending to look at his watch, he continued. "Dinner is scheduled for two o'clock, after which we will have a gift opening extravaganza and a short walk around the deck. The evening entertainment will consist of music by celebrated local artists. We hope you will stay for a light repast and dessert next to the fire. Any questions as to Christmas Day events, please see our concierge." Applaud broke out encouraging Ian to bow.

Ian opened the door for Kat, waiting until she pulled her gown into the car before closing the door behind her. She was a vision. The emerald gown with revealing shoulders had been an extravagant purchase, but he needed one more item to fill her reference book for Fine Evening Attire. He'd found it at a boutique in the historic district. Tonight was the perfect night for it, so he was glad Kat had worn his recommendation.

"You look beautiful, Kat." He leaned over and kissed her cheek. "Looking forward to the concert?"

"I can't wait," she answered. "I'm glad you thought of this, Ian. I miss our old days of jazz hopping and concert nights."

"Tonight will be a real treat. With Zimmerman as the guest conductor, the Schubert and Mozart concert sold out in hours." He pulled

into traffic and began maneuvering his way to 301 Massachusetts Avenue. "And after we've fed our souls," Ian held her hand and smiled a gentle smile, "we'll feed our bodies at L'Espalier where I've made reservations."

Glancing over at Ian, she gently smiled and squeezed his hand. "Thank you for this beautiful evening, Ian. You're a regular Nugent-Harris of Boston. You ever need to moonlight, I think you're concierge skills are second to none."

Chapter 26

GRIZZLY GRATITUDE

The timing of dinner couldn't have been more perfect. It gave the tired an opportunity to take a nap and the more active an opportunity to explore. Ian convinced Emma to show him where some of the gardens had been located. Although she could not pinpoint much, a few ancient trees acted as markers, pointing the way to long lost paths and abandoned gardens. They stood beneath a massive denuded tree with the wind whistling through its limbs. The thick blanket of snow covered everything but memories.

"Emma swing here," Emma pointed out. A low-lying limb was the obvious choice for such an addition. Not only was it the largest tree around, it commanded the longest view. Birch lay behind them to the southeast of Mount Laurel. What lay ahead of them was another town entirely. They could just make out rooftops jutting through the snow and interrupting the tree line. It could have been ten miles away or a hundred, Ian couldn't tell. Regardless, it was a serene view, complete with mountains, trees, and steeples.

He could picture Emma coming here, either with a caretaker or perhaps alone. It wasn't dangerous, other than taking one's breath away. He trudged through the snow to the base of the tree for a more accurate feel. The dogs had beaten him to it, padding down the snow at the base of the tree, revealing some long forgotten chain. Ian pulled it out of its frozen position, following the chain to its end. As he jerked on it, Emma followed the path of the breaking snow. They dug together where it snaked its way from the tree.

"Swing!" sang out Emma. "Emma's swing!"

Eventually the snow was brushed aside to reveal slats and arms to a once useful wooden swing. There was no recovery for this swing; the fasteners long rusted into uselessness and the wood long rotted into earth.

"How often did you come here, Emma?" asked Ian as they piled the debris in a ceremonial heap.

"Emma swing happy here. When sad or mad come here, too."

"Did they put the swing up just for you?"

"Yeah. Papa and Mister Mac put up. If can't find, Emma here." Emma turned to go, history lesson completed.

The dogs happily strolled alongside her, smiling up at her on occasion. She was no stranger to long hikes or snowy climbs. Ian thought she was in better shape than he. He felt winded again, wondering why he'd bothered such a hike.

Before long, Uplands came into view with the brown exterior in stark contrast to the vista of barren winter before it. He wondered what that same view looked like in April, when the silent winter blossomed into the lively cacophony of spring. More than ever he was glad he'd purchased Waltham's Peak and built Uplands. That had been a good choice. Now, if he could just get Kat here.

"Ian, this goose is amazing! I've never had one before, but had I, I know this one would have surpassed them all!" Doc dabbed her mouth with his Scottish linen, wiping away the evidence.

"Thank you for making this meal and this day so special,

Mr. Campbell. I don't know when I've dined in such finery. Even at Waltham's I cooked it, but never enjoyed it like I am today." Ruby reached for a crystal goblet and washed down her squash with a draft of white wine.

After the walk, Ian had set about making the first Christmas at Uplands memorable. While rendering fat and cubing vegetables, he showed the ladies where they could find his linens, china, crystal, and silver. Now, lying before them, was admittedly the best goose he'd ever presented. Combined with the homemade applesauce, yeast rolls, roasted vegetables, and choice wine, it made for a superb meal.

"Bird good," said Emma with a mouthful.

Grinning in spite of himself, Ian thanked them for their compliments.

"My father used to say, 'Eat hearty and give the ship a good name.' He had a grandfather who had been a captain on the great lakes during the Civil War. The expression came from him." His audience was listening intently as they cut tender morsels and savored them. "A ship's reputation had a lot to do with how well they fed their sailors, so he encouraged his sailors to do his advertising for him."

Watching Pearl navigate the parsnips, shallots, pumpkin, artichokes, leeks, and beetroot made Ian laugh.

"What are these, Mr. Campbell? They're super good! Nana?" Pearl didn't wait for a response, "Nana, can we grow these?"

Everyone was excited to see Pearl eating with such fervor. Ruby pointed them out and identified them for Pearl, proving she knew her way around a root cellar.

By the time the meal was eaten, the table cleared, and the dishes washed, it was nigh on four o'clock. They had been leisurely in their meal, caught up again in stories of their respective pasts. Ian listened to lives, very unlike his own, unfold in vivid and lurid detail. Had he been an historian, a blackmailer, or a gambler, he couldn't have been more enraptured.

His own life was beginning to look remarkably innocuous

and predictable in comparison. If they had asked him to share, he could have turned to Doc, asked for her Sherlockian restaurant pronouncements and it would have covered the sum total of his life with as much fanfare as the real thing.

"Pearl, you know what's next on the agenda?"

"Is it presents, Mr. Campbell?" Pearl was beaming. She was the most alive Ian had seen her yet. Her color was brighter, her step lighter, her grin wider. "Who's coming over?"

Ian was confused. "No one, Pearl, it's just us."

"Then who's getting the presents?"

Everyone exchanged looks. For the first time, Ian realized no one, with the exception of Doc, anticipated that the presents were for them.

"I tell you what, Pearl, you go grab a box and tell me what the tag says. Can you do that?"

Pearl looked at him sheepishly. "Yes, sir."

Ian was contemplative as he watched Pearl head for the tree. She brought a package back to him.

"Here you go, Mr. Campbell."

"Thanks, Pearl, now who's it for?" he grinned at her.

"I don't know."

"Well, what does the tag say?"

Understanding evading Pearl, but dawning on Doc, she reached in, held up the tag, and proclaimed, "Pearl! This gift says it's for Pearl!"

"Me? This is for me?" Pearl was mystified.

"It sure does, now open it and let's see what's inside." Ian held it out to her. Pearl stole a glance at her grandmother who smiled back at her.

"Go ahead, Pearl Girl."

Pearl gently pulled apart the paper, clearly unfamiliar with unwrapping presents. She yanked on the ribbon until Doc had to help her with it. Before long, Pearl was holding up a pair of overalls with flannel flowers lining the inside. Tucked beneath them was a light blue turtleneck that matched her shining eyes and the flannel flowers.

"This is for me? I can keep this, Nana?" She grabbed them

to her.

"Of course, sweetheart. That's the way Christmas works, someone makes a sacrifice hoping it'll be appreciated and accepted."

The fresh snowfall could only be seen by moonlight. The power still hadn't come on. As he waited on the porch for the dogs, Ian considered the evening. Finding out that seven year old Pearl couldn't read was a game changer. Somehow, he hadn't expected that. More notable, he hadn't expected it to bother him. The gifts had been a hit. For that, he was thankful, because he took pride in being a good gift buyer.

Dogs done, Ian stepped back into the house. By the time only one package remained beneath the tree, the sun had cast a cool evening shadow. Ian wasn't quite ready for Christmas to be over. He got out his one delicatessen splurge, plum pudding Dickens' style, some hot chocolate and his viola. While the ladies heated water and lighted lanterns, Ian tuned his strings. To strains of Christmas carols, the crude choir sang their way into the night.

Ian held the door for the dogs' last nightly visit.

"Brrr, I think the temperatures are dropping again." He stomped his boots free of snow and closed the door behind him. Doc was seated on the couch nursing the last of her hot chocolate. Waiting for Ian was really her intention. Ian plopped down in a fireside chair eager to roll out his bed.

"Look, Ian, I wanted to tell you what a great thing you did here today. I know I sound like a broken record, and I promise, I don't typically go around affirming people. But you need to know that what you did today was a tremendous blessing." She grinned as she went on, "I'm not just saying this because you got me the coolest Alpaca hat and mitten set I've ever had, either."

Ian couldn't remember the last time, if ever, anyone other than Kat looked at him as intently as Curly Doc for the purpose of saying something nice.

"The pajamas and gardening tools you got Ruby, the blouses and jeans you got Emma, and the overalls and art set you gave Pearl were well thought-out, kind, and generous. Not to mention that you had to race around town like mad to make that happen yesterday. Oh yeah, and while I'm on that topic, how *did* you manage to wash their clothes, buy their presents, and shop for these amazing meals between hospital visits?"

"Just like I told Pearl, Santa and his elves have been there for me." He stifled a yawn and shrugged at her.

"You would have needed the entire population of Whoville to pull off what you've done in the past twenty-four hours."

"I told you, Doc. I'm hired to win."

" Well, good night," she rose to go, "and thank you. It was a fabulous Christmas."

Ian washed up in the downstairs bath, threw on his pajamas, rolled out his bag and checked his phone one last time, congratulating himself for charging it at the laundromat. No calls. No texts. No e-mails. The screen was blank.

The visit was just what MacLean needed. Doc wasn't sure it was the best medicine physically, but she knew taking everyone to see MacLean would be the best medicine for all of them emotionally. Ian had been able to cram all the women in the Range Rover for a quick look-see during visiting hours. When they first walked in, MacLean was a sight. His wispy hair lay matted against his head, saliva dried under his lips. Doc guessed this was the most prone MacLean had been in years. Based on what she'd gathered from the girls, MacLean was an active man keeping all the women in cord wood, and fixing anything and everything for all their homes.

His skin, at one time sunburned and freckled, was as pale as the snow they'd just shaken off their coats. A lack of comprehension and a lack of sleep shone in his eyes.

When Emma came into view, a transfusion took place. Ian was astonished at the visible transformation. Within moments, MacLean was sitting erect, coloring at the effusiveness of his neighbors. Pearl jumped in bed enough to hug MacLean's neck and leave her tears on his cheek. Emma and Ruby each grabbed a hand and riddled him with questions. Yes, he was fine. (*Now*, Ian thought). No, he wasn't in much pain. Yes, he wanted to hate the damned doctors, but he had to admit, they'd come in mighty handy for a change. No, his nurse wasn't pretty and why would anyone ask such a fool question.

Ian and Doc stood back. They both had the sense they were encroaching on a family reunion. The tenderness, the sincere concern for one another, alarmed Ian. He hadn't expected it. He certainly didn't know what to make of it.

"Mister Campbell," Pearl was peering up at him, "can we show Mister Mac? Can we give him his present?"

Grinning, Ian held out a shopping bag to her. Pearl extricated a red-ribboned package, the last one under the tree, bearing the seasonal admonition to "Have a Merry Christmas."

"Lookee here, Mister Mac! A present just for you!" Pearl gently placed the package on the side of the bed, carefully avoiding the bandaged leg.

"Now what fool thing did you all go and do?" MacLean's gruffness couldn't hide his evident emotion.

"Mr. Campbell knows how to shop, Mr. MacLean. I'd open it if I were you," Doc encouraged.

"It's a merry Christmas present, Mister Mac." Emma was grinning more broadly than Ian had ever seen her. Her usual seriousness was replaced with joyful anticipation.

"Yeah! See here, Mister Mac, he got me this!" Pearl stepped back, raised her arms in the air and gave herself a twirl. "Ain't it pretty?"

If ever MacLean was going to lose it, this was it, thought Ian. A quiver was detected in MacLean's lower lip.

"It shore is, Pearl Girl, it shore is." MacLean was grinning at Pearl as if she were his very own.

"Let's see what you've got there, Hamish," piped up Ruby. "The suspense was killin' us all the way here. We've been bettin' on what's in there. If I didn't know you lived on a mountain, I'd swear it was an anchor."

MacLean grabbed the package, but had to adjust his grip when it didn't move. He leaned forward, put a hand underneath and drew it to himself. Staring at the package, he peered up at Ian and took in Emma, Ruby, and Pearl purposely, carefully. His own tear finally pushed its way down his cheek, swirling into the one Pearl had left behind. He leaned back again and addressed Ian.

"Mr. Campbell, I don't know how to thank you."

Ian was uncomfortable. He was ready for thanks for a gift. He had done that sort of thing numerous times and had prepared, rehearsed responses at the ready. What he wasn't ready for was this.

"These girls are all I've got." He was having trouble getting it out. "When I was laid up in that house with the girls sick next door and Emma nursin' us all, I thought we were goners. I figured Emma was up to somethin', but with the snow comin' down like it was, I wasn't gonna let her go. I didn't think there'd be a New Year for any of us, let alone a Christmas."

Ian wanted to sit down. Strange feelings were coming over him he was entirely unused to. For that matter, MacLean wasn't in his element either.

"We been livin' as neighbors for nigh on ten years, Mr. Campbell, but really, we've been family for twenty."

Family. Somewhere deep within Ian, a coolness was overshadowed by something warm and good.

"Ruby and I are the closest thing to siblings either of us has any more. We get on just fine with my choppin', her gardenin' and our mutual efforts. Emma, well, she was born to the Waltham's, but she became mine over time. You might think we're a blessing to her, but the truth of the matter is, Mr. Campbell, she's the blessing to old Ruby and me." MacLean squeezed Emma's hand and turned his head to take in Pearl. "And Pearl Girl here was like new life, a fresh graft on an old vine. At first, we didn't know what to do with the little squirt, but now ... now, we don't know what we'd do without her."

The festive air was gone, replaced by a sweet stillness. Doc was crying. The shimmer on her face gave it away. Ruby and Pearl were taking in MacLean with a calm sense of appreciation. It occurred to Ian that although they had all been living this way for years, MacLean was the first to put to words how much they all meant to each other. He was the first to utter the word "family."

"Emma love Mister Mac." Emma leaned forward and kissed MacLean on the cheek. Clearly, this was unexpected behavior from Emma, for even her "family" was surprised by it. Ruby and Pearl in turn embraced MacLean and wept.

"Look, I'm not much of a family expert," interrupted Ian, but I do know how to do Christmas, and ours won't be complete until you open that package." He had to get this show on the road.

MacLean pulled on the ribbon and allowed Pearl to peel the paper back. It took him some repositioning to pull out the first item. They all laughed to see MacLean unwrap a bright red, four-sided wedge.

"That's mighty nice of you, Mr. Campbell. This'll make my choppin' go a lot faster. My rusty flat one will have to be decommissioned to a door wedge this spring."

"You're not done, Mister Mac!" Pearl peered into the box as MacLean's hands searched for more. The tissue paper was pushed aside to reveal a wool lap blanket with matching tam o' shanter. MacLean slowly picked up the hat, running the dark green plaid over his coarse hands.

"It's the MacLean hunting plaid," informed Ian. "Two hundred years ago, your clan was neighbors with mine, with just a loch between us."

BETSY BOYD LESLIE

Chapter 27

NICK OF TIME

"I don't care if you did drive, I want you to stop at the grocery. It's time I started pulling my own weight around your place."

Doc was insistent. Pearl and Ruby needed to lie down, the day's simple exertions too much for them. But if Doc thought they could take another twenty minutes in the car, then who was he to argue?

"All right, all right, I'll stop. But for the record, you saved their lives. Your weight's already been pulled."

Pearl stirred in Ruby's lap as they wheeled into a spot near the door.

"Keep the heater on. I'll just be a few minutes," and Doc was gone with her backpack slung over her shoulder, her curly hair hiding her profile.

Ruby sat erect in the middle of the back seat, a tired, drawn look on her face. Pearl lay in her lap asleep. Emma was leaning against Ruby's other side, also catching some zees. The sickness, medication, stress, and lack of sleep, had taken their toll on the little family. Naps were still requisite.

"I can't thank you enough for your hospitality, Mr. Campbell." Ruby glanced down at Pearl as she brushed some hair from her cheek, her voice trailing into the front seat.

"Hamish is right. We're all each other have. We have little in the way of earthly possessions, but a lot in the way of good company." Ruby glanced up to meet his gaze in the rear view mirror.

"When Hamish told me he was leaving to get help, I was relieved. Pearl had been ailing for some time, and none of our usual herbs and methods was having any effect." She brushed back more unbidden hair while she thought. Ian preferred the silence. He knew what to do with pauses, even political plaudits, but not sincere appreciation for hazardous duty.

"When I heard that tree go, I knew it would be bad, but had no idea it would be that bad. The hollerin' told me everything I didn't want to know. Me and Emma ran out to see him under that tree and his leg bent back under him. It was awful."

Ruby stopped, choking up over the recent memory. Ian wanted to interrupt her. The narrative was putting him in an awkward place emotionally. This just wasn't his thing. Sterile, impersonal information he could analyze and organize was his thing. This was raw, messy, personal. He shifted in his seat, looking into the windows of the store willing for Doc to come out with the groceries and interrupt them.

"The snow was comin' down so fast and hard that he was covered in it by the time Emma and I pulled him out from under the tree and into his house. I could tell he was in awful pain. Who wouldn't be with his bone stickin' out like that? And then we had to drag him, 'cause we weren't strong enough to pick him up. Not only was he in shock from the blood loss and the break, but by the time we'd gotten him out from under the tree and inside, hypothermia had set in. You can probably guess what the rest of that day and night was like. Between Emma and me, we had to get him warm, clean his wound and dress it, all the while checking on Pearl and helping her. It was the closest to hell I've ever been, Mr. Campbell. Just like Hamish, I figured we were all goners. With Pearl that feverish, Hamish most likely to set in with infection, and me starting to feel the symptoms I'd seen Pearl going through, I thought we were gonna die out there and no one would know 'til someone from town came to check on Emma when she didn't show up for her monthly hair cut."

She looked up again.

"Then you showed up, Mr. Campbell. In the nick of time."

Ian spied Doc's backpack and breathed a sigh of relief. No one could explain the last three days, least of all him. Doc opened the door, jumped into her seat and piled the groceries around her. The snow was coming down again, sheeting the windshield.

"Whew," Doc brushed her hair out of her face, "any longer and we'd have a hard time getting up Waltham's Peak."

"Yeah," Ian tossed the shifter into reverse, "you came out in the nick of time."

Chapter 28

CAMPBELL'S SALAD

"Apparently, you can manage grub just fine." Ian was drying the dishes Doc was handing him and putting them away. Bringing dishes from the table, Emma added her two cents.

"Doc good cook."

"Why, thank you Emma and Ian." Lather dripped from her hands as she set rinsed utensils on a towel. "The truth is, I've got a repertoire of about three meals, and that's the extent of my culinary capabilities."

"Emma make bacon 'n eggs," Emma proclaimed pointing to herself. "Soup, too, Pax and Rex like bacon n' egg leftovers best."

Just having let them out, the dogs had finished the obligatory "rinsing" stage of the supper dishes. Keeping Emma from placing dishes on the floor after a meal would have taken an act of Congress. The others didn't look twice when she'd first placed his fifty-dollar saucer on the floor after a meal, including Doc. Ian had finally come to terms with the fact that Congress was not in session. He'd had to capitulate. Even if he had called a session of Congress, he assumed he'd be vetoed. Most likely they wouldn't understand the concept of a fifty-dollar plate, albeit they'd worked for a man with more. Things were different when one lived *with* the mountains rather than just *in* them, including the pre-wash phase of plate prophylaxis. Things were even more different on Waltham Peak.

"That does it, ladies." Ian draped his damp towel over the range handle. "I don't have a lot of experience in the area of hospitality, so thank you for your help tonight."

He meant it. He and Kat had never entertained much, not because Kat wasn't into hospitality, but because he never approved of anyone enough to let them get past his welcome mat. When it came to just the two of them, he was used to doing it all. Not because Kat didn't pitch in, but because he'd assumed all the kitchen duties after 5:00. He wanted everything done a certain way. Rather than continue to berate and demand, he had simply appropriated the cooking and cleaning that supper entailed.

A different tack had been used for the midday meal. Lunch had been simplified to a particular salad at a particular deli. It was cost effective and simple. Simple in theory. Ian had asked his favorite restaurant to increase the olives by five, switch the lettuce from Iceberg to Romaine, and remove the cottage cheese altogether. They even had a special dressing made to order, which they made and kept for Ian's salads alone. In theory, and for Ian, it was simple. For the restaurant, it was an effort to remain in Ian's good graces.

The staff knew him by name, and had "Campbell's Salad" ready to go every weekday at noon. Shelly simply walked down, signed for it, and took it back to the office. In the event Ian was held up in court or ate out of town, the lunch was placed in the office refrigerator for his supper.

Doc leaned against the Smeg.

"Kat a good cook?" she asked, as Emma took her leave.

"Fair," replied Ian putting the last of the dressing in the fridge.

"Look, I'm not one to pry, but I couldn't help noticing that although you're married, your phone hasn't rung once over the last two days. Days, which for most people would constitute high volume phone usage, even for couples in marital straits."

Ian stood at the door with his hand on the knob. He opened it, stuck his head out and whistled for the dogs. Within moments, two massive forms filled the doorway.

Ian looked back at Doc, "Kat's got her tongue?"

Twinkling lights and bellowing Phil Driscoll provided the perfect complement to Ian's perfectly choreographed evening. Ian fingered the box in his pocket. The Christmas goose he had prepared was delicious. The stroll through Boston Commons was magical. The King's Cake delectable.

On cue, Kat emerged from the bedroom wearing a lovely grey chiffon and a beautiful grin. He had been right to veto Kat's plans and keep Christmas small. Family and friends were too distracting and noisome. This was perfect.

She snuggled up close and he took her in his arms. Her vanilla scent mingled with the cinnamon and pine of the candles Kat had burned earlier in the evening. She felt warm and soft in his arms. He carefully extracted the box and set it on her thigh, the bright letters giving away the luxuriousness of the Tiffany purchase within. Kat stiffened.

"Seeing as how I have emeralds to go with outfits ten through fifteen in Fine Evening Wear; sapphires to go with ensembles six, nine, and sixteen; two pairs of pearls to go with my Daywear Collection; and two pairs of diamonds to go with everything else in the last twenty pages of the outfit guide; I think my current inventory is sufficient." She placed the box in Ian's lap, untucked herself and strode to the bedroom.

"What the hell, Kat," Ian barked as he threw on the bedroom light. "Do you have any idea how much these cost me?"

With her eyes closed and her face enveloped in her pillow she replied, "I don't think you know how much they cost you."

Chapter 29

LEAST LIKELY CANDIDATE

The house phone rang. The first time in days.

"Campbell residence," answered a bleary Doc.

She waited a moment, a look of disbelief overwhelming her features.

"He what?"

"I'm taking 129. I think he'd take the mountain road half way and then strike out by that old garden. That's the only way he can make it on foot, well, on one foot. He knows that."

Ian was throwing on his coat and hat, giving Doc an assessment of his plans more for self-assurance than agreement.

"Ian, I can do this. You stay here with the girls, and I'll find Hamish."

"A," enumerated Ian, "you have no earthly idea where this guy lives. B, you know, as well as I do, that he may be down for the count. C, You don't have the physical strength to load him up and move him out. And D, you even said tonight that the girls weren't out of danger yet. You stay here and keep the home fires burning. I'll find the escapee." He had just finished pulling his hat down around his ears. A quick pat to his leg and a whispered, "here, boy" and Pax was at his side. "It's showtime ... again." With a flourish of keys he was out the mudroom door.

Emma appeared in the kitchen, Rex at her side.

"Where Ian going? Get more groceries?"

"You could say that, Emma, you could say that," Doc mumbled.

They watched Ian back to the end of the gravel, turn his wheels and speed off down the peak. The road was no longer a black ribbon coursing down the mountain, but a mottled grey under the falling snow.

"Emma," Doc whisperingly waked her. "Emma, wake up sweetie."

Rubbing her eyes, Emma leaned on one elbow as she fixed her sleepy eyes on Doc. The room was pitch black, but she could just make out Doc's outline against the moon's rays bathing the room.

"Emma, when you go into town do you walk?" Doc had a sense of urgency that didn't match her question.

"Emma hair cut in town," smiled Emma.

"I know, at Simon's right?" Doc tried to smile the question at her.

"Yes, Simon cut hair 'pixie cute.'"

"He sure does, Emma." Doc sat on the coffee table facing the guest room couch where Emma had fallen asleep waiting for word. "Do you walk there from your house?"

"Yes."

"How long does that take you?"

"Two, three hours. Depends on weather."

"How long does it take you to get from your house to this one?"

"No snow, thirty minutes. With snow, lot more."

Doc was lost in thought as she calculated how long Ian had been gone. Her eyes traveled to the ceiling, taking in nothing but timeframes that didn't add up.

"Ian okay?"

"He got you and Hamish here, didn't he?" Doc tried to sound more confident than she felt. Outright lying had never been her thing, but altruistic deception she could live with.

"Damn mountain man."

Ian was walking toward the porch, frozen snow crunching beneath his feet when Doc approached him. The sun was just coming up, enough to illuminate his swollen sweaty face and raw exposed hands. The car was nowhere to be seen, MacLean was draped over Ian in a fireman's carry. Ian had the energy of a dishrag.

Doc raced back to the front door rather than toward Ian.

"Emma! Emma! Come help me!"

Rex was out the door first, greeting Ian with a sniff rather than the customary wag. He, like Doc, knew something was very wrong. Doc ran to help Ian as he dropped to his knees on the stairs and released his burden. MacLean's head was thrown sideways, intercepted by Doc's thrusting hands. Other than a groan as he succumbed at the stairs, Ian was silent and motionless.

Positioning her arms underneath MacLean's, Doc began to pull him across the porch to the door.

"Emma, grab his feet. We've got to get him inside."

Gently releasing Ian's head to rest on the top stair, Emma got on her feet and went to help Doc. They wrestled him into the house and onto the couch as Rex anxiously circled them, his eyes following the motionless MacLean and searching the moving master's.

"What matter, Doc?" Emma asked as they both stared down at the prone figure.

"I don't know, Emma. Let's go get Ian and we'll take a

closer look."

They both hurried outside to find Ian as he lay, his body spanning the steps. Incoherent words were making their way out of his mouth as Pax sat near his head at the top of the stairs, a look of patient concern on his canine countenance. Doc and Emma carried Ian inside and laid him on the hearth immediately before the fire. Doc stood and rubbed her hands near the fire while Emma closed the door to the increasingly frigid elements. Taking the stairs as quickly as she could, Doc retrieved her medical bag and stethoscope.

She came back downstairs to find Ian wrapped in a blanket, Emma adding wood and stoking the fire. Planting the stethoscope in her ears and wrapping the cuff around Ian's arm was a matter of moments. Emma came close and watched as the needle jerked and slowly spun around the dial. Pax licked her hand and she patted his head reassuringly.

"This isn't looking good, Emma," informed Doc as she looked inside Ian's mouth with a flashlight. Squeezing his arm with a fist, Doc watched the skin slowly regain its shape. She leaned back on her heels and peered up at Emma. Drawing in a deep breath, she made her way over to the couch and repeated all the same procedures with Hamish's body. Moaning and mumbling continued to hail from Ian.

"They've got Scarlet Fever, Emma. The same thing Ruby and Pearl have. They're both dehydrated, too, which would account for such a hard-hitting case in two adults." She stared at the pair, considering the implications and complications of the new diagnosis.

"Doc have medicine," Emma reminded her.

"Not enough, Emma. I brought what I thought Ruby and Pearl would need. I didn't take into account *more* of us getting sick." Doc let her chin fall to her chest.

"Emma get medicine," declared Emma as she made her way to the bottom of the stairs.

"You don't understand, Emma. I don't have enough." Doc turned to see Emma disappearing into the second floor. She raised her voice to be heard.

"There isn't enough up there, Emma. Don't bother!" Doc released a sigh and held her face with her tired hands. She jumped when Emma's voice came from behind her interrupting her thoughts.

"Emma get more medicine."

Doc looked up to see Emma fully clothed for an outing, mittens dangling from her parka sleeves. She was fitting a cap to her head and circling a scarf around her neck.

"Emma, the only two places that have what we need are the hospital and the clinic. You can't go that far on foot. *I* can't go that far," she added, placing emphasis on the pronoun. "Who knows where Ian's car is and mine can't make it in this new snowfall."

"Emma go clinic. Get medicine for Ian and Mister Mac." She stared at Emma's small frame now, decided and determined.

"Emma, I can't let you do that. Since yesterday, we've gotten another six inches of snow and the temperature has dropped. You could die out there."

"Mister Mac and Ian die here," Emma quietly responded.

Doc was stunned. "Ruby, you've got to stop Emma," she panted as she raced into the room, "She's got it in her head that she's going to hike down to town in this ghastly weather to save Ian and MacLean!"

"Whoa, pardner, what's the situation?" asked Ruby as she pulled back the curtains to evaluate the weather. "What's the situation with Hamish and Mr. Campbell, Doc? Just how bad off are they?" She slipped back under the covers and sipped on her water glass. Beginning with the early a.m. phone call from the hospital, Doc explained to Ruby what she knew of MacLean's escape, Ian's rescue, and the pair's current condition.

"I have no idea where Ian found Hamish or what those two have been up to for the past six hours. All I know is that Hamish left the hospital yesterday and Ian found him at some point in the middle of the night and got him here on foot. I'm assuming he abandoned his car because the roads became impassable. Either way, I don't know where his car is and I certainly don't think mine will make it down these mountain roads in this new layer of snow."

"Ian's delirious and feverish. Both can be alleviated with hydration, but of course, his symptoms will continue to worsen until I can get some antibiotics in him. Some of them, as you well know, will continue to run their course, regardless, but no healing will begin until the antibiotics are administered. As for Hamish, he's the one I'm really worried about. His body is fighting off infection from the break, the surgery and now *this*." Doc was sitting in the rocker as she relayed the information. With the prospect of "this" before her, her elbows found her knees and her hands held her head up.

Ruby sighed, drew on reserve strength and reasoned, "Let's say we don't get this medicine into Hamish in the next twenty-four hours. What's the worst case scenario?"

"His infection will be at the point of no return. It would seal his fate." Doc was uncompromising in her response. "The truth is, Ruby, with this setback, he could die anyway." She leaned back and slid down into the rocker. "But if something happened to Emma, we'd have two lives to account for."

"Listen, Doc, you're new to this dynamic, so you don't know Emma well. Even in the short time you've known her, though, you can tell she's up to one thing, and one thing only: helping people. Emma ain't gonna take 'no' for an answer if she thinks she can help in some way. Seems to me we're gonna have one death for sure if she doesn't go or two on the outside, maybe, if she does go." Ruby leaned forward in bed for emphasis.

"Or none, if God is merciful." She relaxed back into bed, surprised at how much the Christmas outing had taken out of her. "She's a big girl. She's done it before. She wants to go. I say you let her go. You ain't the only one gonna save the day, Doc. There are other heroes in this world, however unlikely they may seem."

Tears were streaming down Doc's cheeks. "Am I that bad, Ruby, that I look like I covet the hero role?"

"No, Doc, you're just used to getting that part and you don't know what to do when somebody else ends up cast in it. She'll be okay, Doc. And if she's not, it won't be your fault. Life is just out of our control sometimes. This is one of those times." She grabbed her glass and took another drink.

"Send her up here, Doc, before she goes, so I can kiss her good bye." Ruby reached over and caressed Pearl's sleeping face.

"Ruby, don't you understand? Emma could die out there?"

"Doc, if Emma was a betting girl, she'd lay odds on getting there and back alive. She's been finding her way around this mountain in every kind of weather for the last eleventy years. If anyone can make it, Doc, she can." Ruby gave her a gentle smile. "Besides, aren't those same odds what roped you into this rodeo?"

Doc pushed herself out of the rocker, heavy with emotion, weary with fatigue. She made her way out the door to get Emma, bumping into her as Emma summited the stairs.

Chapter 30

MORE MEDICINE

"Here's your pack, Emma. There's food and water, a headlamp, and some other things you may need. I also wrote a note for you to give the doctor or nurse. It will tell them exactly what we need."

"Thanks, Doc." Emma sounded as if she was headed out the door for a mere walk in the woods. The simplicity of it gladdened and disheartened Doc all at the same time.

"Emma, what you're doing," Doc had to choke back tears, "is very brave and very kind. You know you don't have to go, right?"

"Emma love Mister Mac, and Ian friend. Need medicine, Emma get medicine." It was that simple in Emma's mind: love was action. Every pot of soup heated, every bandage replaced, every trudge over to Ian's, every breakfast of bacon and eggs was that love being played out. Emma opened the mudroom door, stepped aside for Rex and turned to block Pax's exit.

"No, no, Pax. Pax up all night help Ian. Stay here." She patted his head and closed the door.

Doc fell asleep curled up in one of the chairs by the fire. After pouring liquid into both men, injecting all four patients with the remaining antibiotics, staunching a new flow of blood from MacLean's leg, and checking on the girls, she was spent. Even the writhing and moaning form of Ian Campbell couldn't keep her awake any longer. One last glance around the room before she closed her drooping lids revealed the stooping figure of Ruby Grimm. She thanked God someone could rally as she succumbed to her weariness.

"Emma went to get help, didn't she?" Ian was awake and posing the question to Doc.

Ruby's tired, but calm voice intercepted the question. "Doc, I thought it would be okay to give him some ibuprofen. At least it would relieve some of the fever long enough to keep the rest of us sane."

Doc stretched her legs out, noting that she'd been sleeping in the fetal position. Ruby was sitting on the coffee table, an arm's length away from MacLean. She waved a wet cloth in the air, folded it up and placed it on MacLean's sweat-beaded brow. He hadn't stirred since Doc saw him last. How many hours had it been? Two, four, six? The sun seemed to be streaming in the windows from directly overhead, but that could be the reflection off the snow.

Ruby went on, "He's been tossin' and turnin', mutterin' and screamin' like a gov'n'ment worker at a tax audit."

Ruby didn't look so hot herself, but was filling badly needed roles for the troops: nurse and counselor. By the odors emanating from the kitchen, cook too. Ruby swiveled slowly, rose from the table, walked over to Ian and pulled the askew blankets up around his shoulders.

"Yes, Emma's gone. We've already got 'help,' thanks to yours truly," she cut her eyes to Doc, "so she's just getting more medicine to top us off. In the meantime, you're to remain calm, keep head and arms inside your blankets at all times and heed the advice of your caretakers. Now, drink this."

Ruby thrust a glass of water at Ian anticipating full compliance. No one had to say "drink" twice. Ian felt like he could swallow a lake. His temperature, thirst, and throat were all demanding quenching.

"I sure needed that," sighed Ian as he handed the glass back to Ruby.

Doc rubbed her eyes and sat up.

"Thank you, Ruby, for taking care of things. I know you're not quite up to it yet, so I'll send you back to bed now that I've gotten some zees under my belt. What's that delicious smell?"

"That, my friend, is the best homemade soup on this side of Waltham Peak. I'll dish some up and get you back on your feet before I get off mine."

"From what I can gather, Doc, I'm now one of the Scarlet Fever statistics. If I wasn't before, I'm now delusional and may regress when this latest drug wears off or runs out. So, before I lose my mind again, would you mind telling me how the least likely candidate for finding a clinic in the driving snow and coming back alive was drafted for the job?" Ian wasn't angry, but he had a definite edge to his voice as he spoke.

Guiltily, Doc looked across at him as he leaned back into the chair for support.

"Look, Ian, it wasn't my idea. I tried to talk her out of it. I tried to convince Ruby to talk her out of it. The truth is, *I* was out of it." She set her soup bowl down and got up to check MacLean's. She wasn't fully caught up, but more sleep would have to wait. "Hamish is on the brink of death. His body was already fighting the break infection, then it had to face a surgery and threat of infection from that. And now it's finally succumbed to this superbug of a Scarlet Fever virus. Whatever resistance his body had before, has completely vanished. Yours too, for that matter. Since he's no longer in the hospital receiving intravenous antibiotics, he's got nothing left to fight with. Any good bacteria or antibodies he had are gone, killed off in the strafing of the antibiotics. I did give the two of you the last of the antibiotics I had, so he's got a fighting chance." She turned to look at him. "But it's a small chance."

"Then there's you. Same goes. Typically, Scarlet Fever doesn't show up in adults. But," she caught her breath, "because of your continued exposure and the physically and emotionally stressful conditions you've been in the last several days, your body could no longer resist whatever awful strain this is. Dehydration and hypothermia didn't help. Your body basically shut down last night. We had to carry you in the house and you've been feverish and delirious ever since. So, *your* immediate future is in Emma's hands, too."

"If I could rant and rave right now, I would." Ian was becoming more agitated by the moment. He was simply too weak to put up a fight, either verbally or otherwise. "She shouldn't be out there, Doc! She can't do it, and then she'll die – because of us." Doc wasn't sure, but his voice seemed to quiver.

With more confidence than she felt, Doc offered, "Ruby seemed to think she could do it. She reasoned that even if she couldn't, I had to leave it up to Emma. Right or wrong, that's what I did. She's a pretty determined person when it comes to helping others."

Ian looked stricken.

"Tell me about it," Involuntarily, he hugged himself to fight off chills. The fire raged next to him and from within. He could feel the ibuprofen wearing off. He wasn't big on medicine, over the counter or otherwise, so he was sure there wasn't much in the house. He was surprised Ruby had found any.

"Emma's been coming to my house every morning for the past two months." His burden had become unbearable. "It's inexplicable, but she makes me bacon and eggs every morning. I mean *every* morning. Since the first day I arrived here until three days before this whole thing started, she's been showing up in my kitchen at promptly six a.m. That's how I knew something was wrong. No matter how hard I tried, I could not get her to stop coming and cooking. I've tried locking her out, yelling at her, unplugging appliances, emptying my fridge, you name it. I didn't know what to do with her or how to get rid of her. I just knew I wanted her out of my kitchen – out of my life."

Now he was outright shivering and sweating. His tongue was swelling and his head was swimming. He had to get this out before it made him sicker than he already was.

"I felt terrible when I found her taking care of her friends. Apparently, that's what she does, that's who she is. All she'd ever done was show me kindness and here I was constantly pushing her away. It wasn't changed locks or bad treatment that kept her away. The only thing that stopped her from coming to my house was a need greater than mine." He couldn't control himself any more. The sobs shook his body.

"In some sick way, I think I thought by helping her friends we would be even and I wouldn't have to feel bad for how I'd treated her. I was wrong." He made one final effort. "I was wrong with Kat, and wrong with Emma. I'm sorry. I'm so sorry."

With that, Ian curled up in the fetal position at the foot of the fire. The silent noise of Ian's sadness wedged itself between wholeness and emptiness.

Doc pushed a pillow under Ian's head and brought the blanket about his shoulders as he slipped out of consciousness.

"Hey!"

Ian felt a tug at his shirt. He turned to face the most beautiful girl he'd ever seen.

"I've been trying to catch up with you since the admin building."

Whoever the lovely apparition was, she was out of breath. She pursed her lips and breathed through them slowly to catch her breath. Ian waited, curious as to the interruption.

"You dropped this outside the admin building. These fell out, too."

She thrust his wallet at him with sundry cards and cash.

Recognizing the wallet, Ian took from her what she offered and checked to make sure everything was accounted for.

"It's all there," the girl added when she realized what he was doing. "It took me a minute to gather them up, which is why you got so far ahead of me."

"Wow, I can't thank you enough. Who knows what would have happened if you hadn't been a good Samaritan. This is my bank withdrawal which was going to cover next semester's books." Setting his backpack on the ground, he took a moment to reassemble his wallet.

"Thanks again, for doing this. Not many folks you can trust these days with a wallet full of identity and cash. If you hadn't come along, who knows what my next several months would have looked like trying to get my identity back."

"Speaking of identity, based on your college ID, you're Ian Campbell." She thrust out her hand, "According to my student ID, I'm Katherine Sommers, but you can call me Kat."

"Nice to meet you, Kat. I'm, oh yeah, we covered that. I owe you. Can I make it up to you with a cup of coffee or a bite to eat?" He glanced at his watch. I can walk you back to your dorm, and if we plan it right, we can hit Frenchy's before the big rush."

"You know, that sounds great. I came in to town to see a friend of mine only to find her down with the flu. She doesn't want me getting it so she's kicked me out. I was heading back to Williamsburg after I dropped off this NyQuil and gingerale. How about we head that way together, I drop these off, and you can show me what Frenchy's is all about."

Ian grabbed the shopping bags she was carrying, noting the infirmary she had purchased.

"Well, if you've got all weekend and you're not from around here, I'll show you what Charlottesville is all about."

"Hello, is this Katherine Sommers of *Sommerset Studio?*"

"Yes it is."

"This is Dr. Laura Tate of Mount Laurel, North Carolina. I need to speak to you about your husband." The silence, although not unexpected, certainly wasn't welcome. "Hello?"

Kat looked out the window at the sleepy cypress swaying with the warm evening breezes. "Yes, I'm still here."

"Mrs. Campbell, your husband is in the hospital and is in his second week of a coma. He is sick with a vicious and virulent strain of Scarlet Fever." She paused, waiting for a comment from the other end of the line. When there wasn't one, she glanced over at Ian's sleeping form and continued. "As his closest living relative, I need to ask you a few questions. Do you have a few moments?"

"What is his prognosis, Doctor?" Came the quiet reply.

"I expect him to pull through, but there is an outside chance this will get the best of him. The next 48 hours will be most telling. Even if he does survive, you need to know, there may be permanent damage." Doc took in Ian's visage as she delivered this last piece of news. To her surprise, tears were coursing down his cheeks.

THE END

BETSY BOYD LESLIE

ABOUT THE AUTHOR

BETSY BOYD LESLIE is a native of Tampa, Florida, where she currently lives with her husband, four children, two parents, two dogs, and a cat. Although she managed the cuckoo clock department of her father's clock shop, practiced as a prosecuting attorney at the county courthouse, and served as an adjunct professor at a local university, she has found marriage and parenting far more rewarding occupations. Enjoy her fiction debut with this first volume in the Waltham's Peak series.